A Guide to Parliamentary Enclosures
in Wales

A Guide to Parliamentary Enclosures in Wales

JOHN CHAPMAN

UNIVERSITY OF WALES PRESS
CARDIFF
1992

© University of Wales, 1992

All rights reserved. No part of this book may be reproduced, stored in a retrieval system, or transmitted, in any form or by any means, electronic, mechanical, photocopying, recording or otherwise, without clearance from the University of Wales Press, 6 Gwennyth Street, Cardiff CF2 4YD.

A catalogue record for this book is available from the British Library

ISBN 0-7083-1111-3

Artwork kindly supplied by the author.

Printed in Great Britain by Billings, Bookplan, Worcester.

CONTENTS

Foreword	1
Introduction	3
Abbreviations	22
County Summaries	23
Anglesey	24
Breconshire	30
Caernarfonshire	41
Cardiganshire	49
Carmarthenshire	58
Denbighshire	73
Flint	88
Glamorgan	101
Merionethshire	108
Monmouthshire	113
Montgomeryshire	121
Pembrokeshire	134
Radnorshire	140
Directory of Welsh Enclosure Commissioners	158
Bibliography	180
Appendix: Irish and Scottish Enclosures	183
Index of Places Enclosed	185

FOREWORD

The need for a guide to the Parliamentary enclosures of Wales was brought home to me by painful personal experience. In 1974, dissatisfied with the existing published statistics of the enclosure movement, I set out to obtain a statistically-valid sample of the awards for England and Wales in order to attempt an up-dating of the figures. In England, the task was relatively straightforward. For well over half the counties, W. E. Tate had already published a list; for most of the remainder, alternatives by other authors were in print. In only a handful of cases, notably the North Riding of Yorkshire and Norfolk, was there no source to turn to. For Wales, however, the situation was very different. Bowen's major compilation from 1914 listed only the Acts, not the associated awards, and was in any case incomplete. Dodd's lists covered only parts of north Wales. Worse still, the absence of county record offices in Breconshire, Radnorshire, and Montgomery meant that comprehensive manuscript or card-index lists were not readily available either. Faced with this situation, I had no alternative but to attempt to do for Wales what Tate had done for England: to match the individual Acts in the British Library and the House of Lords Record Office collections with the various awards scattered over a wide range of repositories in both England and Wales. By the time my sampling was completed in 1982, Michael Turner had taken up Tate's work, and the whole of England, plus Monmouthshire, was covered in published form in the *Domesday of English Parliamentary Enclosures*. The rest of Wales has remained a blank, and it seemed that it might be helpful, and might save other researchers a great deal of unnecessary work, if the results of my investigations could be made available in published form.

This guide was thus conceived as a companion volume to the *Domesday*, and the definition of such matters as what constituted "an enclosure" was adopted so as to be consistent with it. However, the actual presentation of the information has been varied in a number of respects. Tate's basic division of his lists into enclosures which affected open field and those which did not is a potentially misleading one even for England; for Wales, where few contained any arable and in those which did the proportion was often very small, such a division would have been totally inappropriate. Tate also chose to list his enclosures by date, and while such a procedure is perfectly logical it is not necessarily the most helpful one for the local historian, who is envisaged as one of the principal users of this volume. The decision was taken to list simply by alphabetical order of parish for each of the historic counties of Wales, as being the form most likely to be of the greatest use to the largest number of individuals.

The very small number of Welsh enclosures, by comparison with those of England, offered the opportunity of including additional information without making the guide excessively large and cumbersome. It is therefore more detailed than the *Domesday*, with more specific descriptions of the lands concerned and with some information on the individuals involved, either as proprietors or as major officials in the enclosure process. Such information is of necessity incomplete, both for reasons of space and of the inadequacy or complexity of the enclosure documents. It is hoped that the inclusion of this material, partial as it may be, will help local users to see their own results in a broader context, and perhaps encourage them to fill in some of the gaps left by this volume.

This work could not have been compiled without the willing assistance of the county archivists and staff of all the Welsh county record offices, many of whom offered detailed comments on my early drafts, and of the staffs of the National Library of Wales, the Public Record Office, the British Library, and the House of Lords Record Office. To all of these I owe a considerable debt of gratitude. I am particularly indebted to Mr R. Morgan, the newly appointed archivist for Powys, for his helpful and encouraging comments, and to Dr Colin Thomas, of the University of Ulster, for drawing my attention to a number of errors and omissions.

I am also grateful to the Social Science Research Council, as the E.S.R.C. was then called, for the grant which financed much of the travel inevitable in this work, and to Dr Trevor Harris, formerly my research assistant, who aided me with the data collection. Credit for the drawing of the maps lies with Mr Bill Johnson, of the Cartographic Unit of the Portsmouth Polytechnic Department of Geography. Finally, my thanks are due to the anonymous reader on behalf of the Board of Celtic Studies for the helpful suggestions on the method of presentation of the information.

INTRODUCTION

The principal object of this volume is to provide a handlist of the Parliamentary enclosures of Wales, but it seems appropriate to provide some context for the bald listing by means of a brief survey of the movement as a whole.

Parliamentary enclosure is normally defined merely as an enclosure carried out under the direct authority of an Act of Parliament, but such an apparently clear-cut definition nevertheless leaves scope for doubt and minor differences of interpretation. For the vast majority of enclosures undertaken before 1836 there is normally no problem, for there was usually an individual authorizing Act specifying which lands were to be enclosed. In England, a few early Acts were merely retrospective confirmations of earlier enclosures by agreement, but they appear in the so-called Blue Books of 1904 and 1914 (Parliamentary Papers, 50, 1904, and 399, 1914) and have been accepted as genuine Parliamentary enclosures by most major authorities (see, for example, Slater, 1896, and Turner, 1978). In the specific case of Wales, the point is an academic one, for there appear to be no examples there of purely confirmatory enclosures.

From 1836 onwards the position is more difficult. The legislation of 6 & 7 Wm IV c.115, 1836, and 3 & 4 Vic. c. 31, 1840, offered blanket authorization for enclosure by agreement, providing that the land concerned contained some open arable and that certain other conditions were met, notably support by the owners of at least two-thirds of the land. Such enclosures therefore lack a formal starting point, consisting solely of an award, but are normally regarded as 'Parliamentary' (e.g. Turner, 1978). The logic of including these, while excluding those under 29 Geo. II c.36, 1756 and its amendment under 31 Geo. II c.41, 1757, which authorized limited enclosures for timber-growing by mutual consent, is open to question. Again, however, Wales appears to have had no enclosures under either of these pieces of legislation.

From 1845 (8 & 9 Vic. c.118) onwards Parliament resumed control over the enclosure process through the medium of 'Inclosure Commissioners' (1), who vetted schemes on Parliament's behalf, and from 1852 each enclosure was again subject to individual authorization, though normally now as one of a batch presented in a single Act by the Commissioners. Subsequent legislation, however, served to confuse the issue once more, for the Commons Act of 1876,

1. Not to be confused with the earlier commissioners, who carried out the actual division of the land in the field. The 'Inclosure Commission' delegated the division to 'valuers'.

and various later amendments, left the Commissioners responsible for regulation schemes and schemes involving mere exchanges of enclosed land, as well as enclosures, and it is not always clear into which category some later schemes should rightly fall. Many Welsh commons were dealt with under this legislation, and a few disputable cases are mentioned in the guide. The award for Twyn Trewan (Anglesey), for example, appears amongst the enclosure awards, but seems not to have involved any element of enclosure and has been disregarded here; on the other hand, the various awards for Coity Wallia (Glamorgan, nos. 53003 and 53013), though somewhat unusual, do seem to have resulted in some enclosure of open common, and have therefore been included. There are also a number of more modern schemes, for example for road-building, which technically involved enclosure but which are very different in kind and usually involve only a very small acreage. Reference has been made to those taking place prior to the Second World War, but they have not been given a formal enclosure number or included in the maps. In general, wherever problems of definition have arisen the attempt has been made to adopt the same criteria as those laid down by W. E. Tate (Turner, 1978), thus ensuring, as far as possible, consistency and comparability with other modern work on enclosure.

Using these definitions, the Parliamentary enclosure movement spanned a period of over 300 years, and affected all four countries of the United Kingdom as constituted at that time. The Scottish legal situation was such that Parliamentary enclosures were not normally considered necessary, but for reasons which remain obscure even Scotland had one Act, that for Falkland and Strathmiglo in Fife in 1815. Ireland had a thin scattering, at least thirteen being passed after the union of the parliaments in 1801 (See Appendix I). The great bulk, however, were concentrated in England and Wales, some 5341 affecting the former and 229 the latter. In terms of dates, the first such enclosure is generally accepted as that for Radipole, Dorset, in 1604, but the movement did not begin in earnest until the eighteenth century, when it was adopted as the normal method of enclosure in the English Midlands, spreading rapidly to other areas. During the 1720s and 1730s many Acts were merely confirmatory, but by the 1750s they had become the principal means of initiating new enclosures, at least as far as open arable land was concerned.

The use of Acts to initiate waste enclosures took longer to become firmly established, even though the earliest ones had been for this purpose. Though the habit spread rapidly from field to waste enclosures in the English Midlands, there was a time-lag, increasing with distance from this area, before it was adopted with enthusiasm elsewhere (Chapman, 1987). Enclosure by agreement always offered an alternative, and while this seems to have been rapidly abandoned for field-land after 1750, it remained a significant feature of many regions into the nineteenth century as far as waste enclosure was concerned. Much of the waste enclosure of Monmouthshire, for example, was carried out without Parliamentary sanction, and indeed often by tacit, rather than formal agreement (Chapman, 1972).

In these circumstances, it is hardly surprising that Welsh enclosures were, characteristically, late. The general rarity of open fields there by 1750 meant that it did not join in the early wave of field enclosures to any significant degree, and it may be suggested that this in itself was a further factor in the late adoption of the Act as the normal means of accomplishing waste enclosures. Unfamiliarity with the Parliamentary processes may have been a major deterrent to local landowners, and lack of experienced local men to draw upon as enclosure officials was probably even more significant. It is very noticeable that the earliest Monmouthshire enclosures recruited experienced commissioners from a considerable distance away, rather than relying upon local men as was the norm, presumably because the appropriate expertise was not available. The absence of 'professional' commissioners in Wales at an early date also meant that there was no body of men with an incentive to encourage landowners to undertake Parliamentary enclosure schemes, a role which such commissioners undoubtedly played elsewhere.

For whatever reason, although there was a Welsh Parliamentary enclosure as early as 1752 (Dee Estuary, 52003), there were only thirteen before 1790, and over 50 per cent took place after 1840. The peak of the Welsh movement was thus getting on for a century later than that in the core area of the English Midlands, and noticeably lagging behind neighbouring English counties such as Gloucestershire.

As Map 1 shows, this is something of a generalization, for within Wales itself there were marked variations. Much of the enclosure of Flint and the adjacent areas of Denbighshire was begun during the twenty years from 1790 to 1810, largely coincident with the Napoleonic Wars, but in many other parts this period, one of major activity in a good deal of England, produced only a small scattering of Acts. In contrast, Radnorshire and Breconshire show a very high concentration in the period after 1850, and Parliamentary enclosure was to all intents and purposes a product of the legislation of 1845. While rational explanations may be offered for these variations at a general level, they are not always very convincing when examined in more detail. For example, it may be argued that late enclosures, after 1845, were principally concerned with scraps of land too small to justify the expense of enclosure by individual private Act, or with large areas of waste where the land was believed to be of such poor quality that, once again, the expense could not

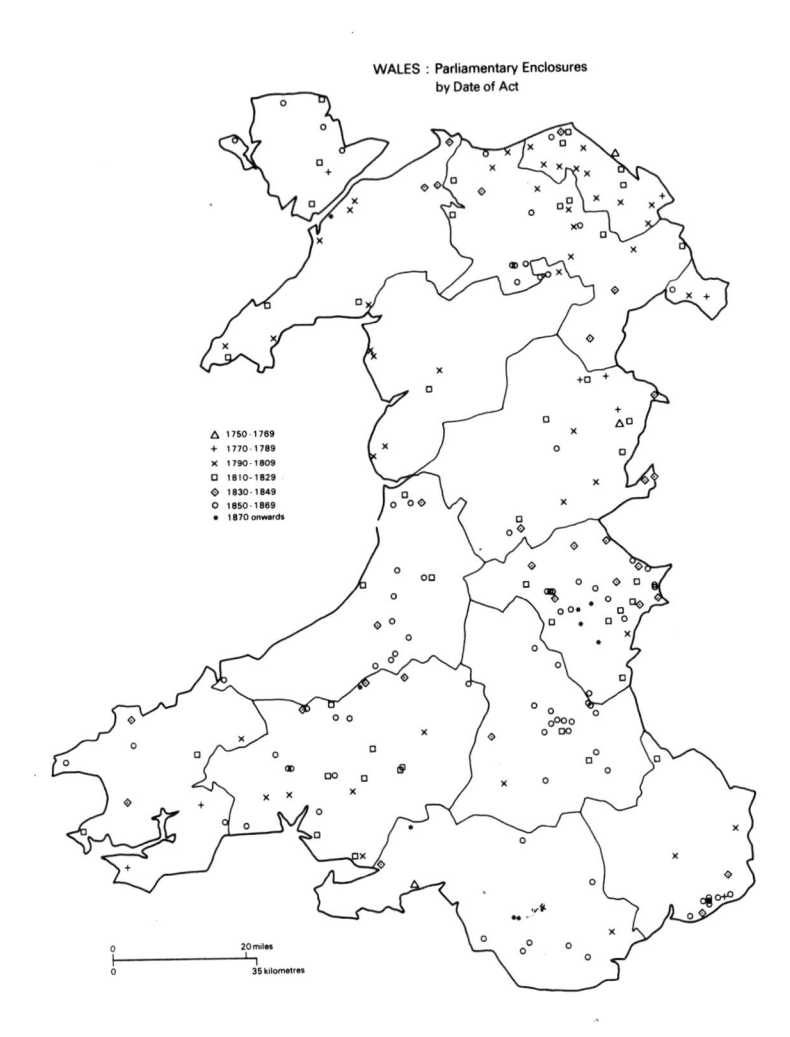

WALES : Parliamentary Enclosures
by Date of Act

△ 1750-1769
+ 1770-1789
× 1790-1809
□ 1810-1829
◇ 1830-1849
○ 1850-1869
• 1870 onwards

0 20 miles
0 35 kilometres

WALES: Known Parliamentary Awards by Date

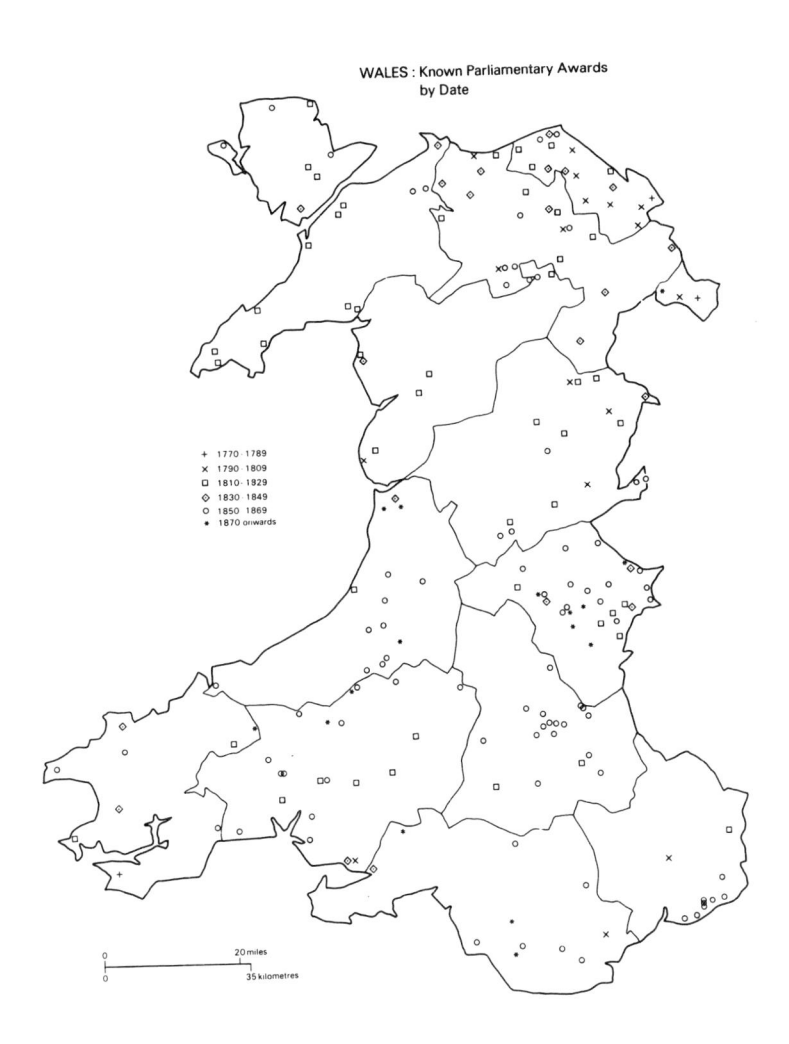

+ 1770-1789
× 1790-1809
□ 1810-1829
◇ 1830-1849
○ 1850-1869
• 1870 onwards

be justified. The former would accord well with most of the late Brecon enclosures, and the latter with many of the Cardiganshire ones. However, if this were the sole explanation it would be difficult to account for many of the large Caernarfonshire awards which occurred at a relatively early date, though the land quality can have appeared no better, and it is even more difficult to explain why Monmouthshire failed to tackle its open fields before the 1850s. There is clearly a need for an examination of the role of the major landowners, of their financial resources, of their other commitments, and of their attitudes to the running of their estates, for the key to many of the local anomalies may lie with them.

A further characteristic feature of many Welsh enclosures was the long gap between Act and award. Though a few English awards took many years to complete, anything over five or six was unusual, yet many Welsh awards dragged on for far longer (compare maps 1 and 2). Again, an explanation might be sought in the exceptional complexity of a substantial minority of Welsh enclosures, involving multiple claims by many individuals for properties and rights scattered across several townships. The fact that the areas involved were often large, poorly mapped, and of dubious quality must also have slowed down the process. However, English awards of equal complexity rarely took so long, and the inexperience of Welsh commissioners may once more have been a factor. Certainly examples of unnecessarily complex or muddled awards are not unusual (see, for example, Llanarthne, 50009, Carmarthenshire), and some required subsequent correction of major errors (for example, Abergwili, 50001). There were also an unusual number of cases where commissioners had to be replaced for inaction or incompetence. It is difficult to resist the conclusion that a number of men were drawn by the money to be made as a commissioner, but rapidly lost interest when it became obvious how much work was involved.

It is also true that many Welsh enclosure commissioners chose to break up the work, dealing with each township separately, and often producing and signing each award as it was completed. Thus the initial award under a particular Act might be finished, and the allotments released to the new owners, as much as a decade or more before the last one. Such a division of the area was by no means unknown in England, but was much less frequent, even where land of comparable acreage and quality was involved. In these circumstances the pressure on the commissioner to complete the job may have been greatly reduced, for many of the major landowners would have been able to start work on parts of their new lands, and may have been quite happy to tackle the problems over a number of years, rather than being forced to commit their energies and financial resources to all of the areas at the same time. In this respect the delays may have had results similar to the system of 'permissive' enclosures, widely used in north Yorkshire but rare in Wales (Chapman, 1976; Edwards, 1963), which permitted the absorption of large tracts of waste to be undertaken in easy stages.

Parliamentary enclosures in Wales thus tend to differ somewhat from the norm for England, though the degree to which this was so should not be overstressed. They operated under the same general legislation and rules, and some of both the landowners and the commissioners were involved in enclosures on both sides of the border. Moreover, though the Welsh enclosures differ greatly in terms of the type of land and farming system affected from those of the English Midlands, the same is much less true of the enclosures of many other parts of England. The small, late waste enclosures of Breconshire can be matched by those of Cornwall, and the vast tracts of moorland of Caernarfonshire by those of north Yorkshire and Northumberland. The differences are perhaps more subtle and more localized than may at first appear.

The Enclosure Process and its Records

Parliamentary enclosure, though officially sanctioned by Parliament in London and subject to certain constraints laid down by it, was essentially a local process. It was initiated by those with an interest in the locality concerned and, within broad guidelines, what was done was determined by these local interested parties. This applies equally to the record which was kept, so there is substantial variation in the volume and nature of the documentation from one enclosure to the next. Only in the late nineteenth century is there something approaching standardization, in the records now held in the MAF collections of the Public Record Office.

Precisely who initiated any particular enclosure is often difficult to determine. Certainly by the time that the process was commonly adopted in Wales any reasonably well-informed landowner or land agent must have been aware of its existence, and the possibility of adopting it must have been discussed informally in many places. Such discussions might have gone on for many years before any formal action was taken (as at Amberley, Sussex. See Chapman, 1980, pp.85-6), and, indeed, might ultimately never have been pursued (for example, Bedwellty, Monmouthshire. See Hassall, 1812, p.68). Records of this phase are inevitably very rare, and are often best where there was an absentee landowner, who had to be consulted by letter; where all were locals, it is unlikely that anything was normally committed to paper at this stage.

In order to stand a chance of success, a proposal needed the support of the owners of at least two-thirds of the land, and an advertisement in a local newspaper of a meeting to gauge the level of support is often the first indication that an enclosure was projected. Again, however, this was not essential, especially if informal discussions had indicated that adequate support was already assured. In that case, the next stage would be to instruct an agent, usually a local solicitor, to draw up a draft enclosure bill for consideration by the interested parties. Again, the initial draft rarely survives, nor does any comment upon it. Wales, however, is particularly fortunate here in that the Crown had an interest in many enclosures, and brief written comments by the Crown agents do survive, normally in the CREST collection in the Public Record Office. Even these are usually no more than a simple note that the Crown's interests seem adequately covered, and proposals for the appointment of an assistant commissioner to watch over the award on the Crown's behalf.

It was only when the finished bill was presented to Parliament, usually by a local MP, that any formal record had to appear. Even then the extent of the record may be extremely brief. The bill had to pass through the usual procedures of three readings in each House, with detailed consideration in committee, but the Journals of both Houses may be tantalizingly uninformative. Thus the Horsham, Sussex, minutes specify that the committee rejected one of the original nominees as commissioner, but who was rejected, and why, is not recorded (Chapman, 1982). Amendments were indeed frequent, but whether these were normally mere technicalities or matters of substance cannot be determined. The first available record to throw any significant light on most enclosures is thus the Act as eventually passed. Copies of all Acts are available at the House of Lords Record Office, and copies of the Printed ones, plus some of those technically Not Printed, are held in the British Library. Odd copies of some have also found their way to various record offices and libraries, but no single collection exists which approaches a comprehensive cover of any county. Furthermore, some of the copies are in reality copies of the bill, with information missing, or which was changed before the Act was passed.

The passing of an enclosure Act was no guarantee that any further proceedings would take place, or that they would leave any record if they did. In a small number of cases, for example Caernarfon (48005), no division of the land was necessary since the Act specified that the land concerned was to be taken over by some body, usually a local authority or body of trustees, and detailed the compensation to be provided for any commoners or other interested parties. No award was necessary, and the Act itself was the end of the process. There were also cases where the Act, once passed, was not proceeded with. Why this was so is not always clear, nor is it always easy to determine whether an enclosure was abandoned, was begun but not completed, or was completed but has left no award. Thus there appears to be no evidence that the Llanddarog (50010) Act was ever followed up, while for St Clears (50028) a map signed by the commissioners survives, but no trace has been found of the accompanying award.

The descent of the commissioner or commissioners upon the community concerned in order to carry out the enclosure produced the greatest variations of all in the record. Initially there was no requirement for the commissioners to make any formal record of their meetings, and even later, when minutes had to be taken, there was no compulsion to retain them once the enclosure had been legally completed. Rodgers records that some Yorkshire Acts made provision for the minute books to be preserved in a specified safe place (Rodgers, 1962), but this was by no means usual elsewhere. Thus minutes for many enclosures may never have existed, and those which did may have been destroyed long ago. Where they do exist, they may vary from the briefest note that a meeting took place to consider claims or inspect the land, to detailed accounts of the proceedings, sometimes accompanied by copies of claims, objections, letters and accounts. Often the best records of this stage may occur in the papers of the individual estates involved, for they frequently kept copies of material sent to the commissioners, and where an agent was acting for an absentee landowner correspondence between owner and agent may throw much light on the details of events. Inevitably, however, it is usually for the larger estates that such material survives, and it is not necessarily very representative of the general picture.

The award itself was the ultimate outcome of the enclosure process, where it was successfully completed, and as a legal document recording ownership of land would seem at first sight to be one which would have been worthy of special care. In practice, as has already been indicated, a significant number seem to have vanished in the intervening period. Though, as a rule, it was stated in the Act that copies had to be deposited in specified places (for Wales usually the parish chest and/or with the Clerk of the Peace of the relevant county) this requirement seems to have been widely ignored. Particularly during the period of the Napoleonic Wars and immediately afterwards, a number of awards seem to have remained in the hands of the clerks to the enclosure, usually local solicitors, and it is these which are now often impossible to trace. Unfortunately this appears to have been especially prevalent in Wales, and the proportion of awards missing is substantially higher than in England.

Though the contents of the awards were to some extent constrained by their inherent purpose, the variations in them go beyond mere quirks of presentation. Some omitted details of old enclosed land which was exchanged or reallocated by the award; some give no details of the prices received where land was sold at auction to raise the costs of the enclosure; some even fail to specify the individuals to whom the land was allotted, recording occasional allotments as being awarded to 'The Owner'. There is thus no guarantee that comparable information can be extracted from the awards even where they have survived intact.

The award was not always the end of the process, for the commissioner's verdicts were open to challenge either in the courts or through bodies of arbitrators, and these options were occasionally taken up by aggrieved individuals or groups. It was even possible for the whole award to be overthrown, as happened at Llanfechell (46004), where Richard Wakeford Attree, one of the most experienced of all the commissioners to operate in Wales, resigned in the face of hostility to his original award, and a new one was drawn up by a new commissioner. More usually, amending awards merely corrected or clarified minor details of the original. Once this had been done, official legal interest in an enclosure ceased, and no further records were maintained. For the long-term results of enclosure, therefore, it is necessary to turn to private collections, the details of which are beyond the scope of this volume.

The Form of the Listings

While it is the aim of this guide to present the enclosures in as uniform a manner as possible, the nature of the material, particularly the awards, makes total uniformity impossible. As has already been indicated, at least until 1845 Parliamentary enclosures were essentially local matters, and although Parliament from time to time laid down certain ground rules, the way in which the material was presented and the type of information included in the documentation was largely at the whim of the commissioners and the clerks. What some felt was essential information, others regarded as totally unimportant. Since commissioners normally worked within a fairly restricted area, and it was usual to employ a local solicitor as clerk, enclosure awards tend to take on a regional flavour at any particular period, so that, for example, a Dorset award of the late eighteenth century differs in style of presentation from a contemporary one from Hampshire. Though this is less marked in Wales, where the small number of enclosures at any given period offered less opportunity for the development of local traditions, it is nevertheless detectable.

Such variations sometimes go further than minor points of style, and affect the type of information which this guide is attempting to present. The surveyor, for example, is frequently not named, and while this is sometimes because one or other of the commissioners undertook this role, there were undoubtedly cases where a separate surveyor was employed but not recorded in the formal documents. This can sometimes be discovered from the various associated papers which have survived, but in others the surveyor's identity has had to remain blank. Treatment of the information on roads is also highly variable, with some commissioners specifying the area of land involved whilst others give only the width and location. Similar problems affect many of the other items of information, even if only in a few odd awards.

LOCALITIES AND PLACE-NAMES

The form of presentation of the listings was determined by the perceived need. It was felt that the majority of users were likely to approach it from an interest in a particular locality, and hence from a desire to discover which enclosure or enclosures affected that place. The primary presentation is therefore alphabetically by parish, the unit most likely to be familiar to local researchers and readily identifiable by those less familiar with an area. Where land in more than one parish was affected by a particular enclosure this has been noted, and the other parishes cross-referenced in the alphabetical list. In this case, the enclosure has been listed under the parish in which the majority of the land lay, if this could be readily determined, or otherwise under the one listed first in the relevant Act or award. Where either the Act or award is habitually referred to by some other name in, for example, the Public Record Office or County Record Office listings, this too has been cross-referenced, so that the user working from such listings can relate it to the appropriate parish. Each separate enclosure has been allocated a reference number, consisting of a two-digit suffix relating to the historic county followed by a three-digit number unique to that particular enclosure. These numbers refer to the author's computerized listings of all English and Welsh enclosures, and have been reproduced here as an aid to internal cross-referencing, and also in the hope that they may offer a helpful form of shorthand for future scholars.

The spelling of place-names presented a dilemma, for the modern standardized spellings of Welsh names frequently differ considerably from those commonly used in the past, and it is the latter which are most liable to be the ones found in the eighteenth- and nineteenth-century documents with which this guide is principally concerned. There was, furthermore, the vexed question of parallel

English and Welsh names, both correct within the context of their own languages, and ranging in differences from the minor spelling variations of the Cardiff/Caerdydd pair to those from totally different roots, as in the Swansea/Abertawe one. The final decision reflects a concern for utility rather than consistency. Since the principal aim is to guide the user from a known modern place to unknown enclosure documents, it seemed most appropriate to present the parish names in their modern form, while retaining the minor names in the form in which they may be found in the contemporary documents, and in which the searcher is therefore likely to find them. Such a solution was also attractive to one with only the most limited knowledge of the Welsh language. As Elwyn Davies points out in his Gazetteer, 'the pitfalls of popular etymology are neither fewer nor less deep in Welsh than in any other language' (Davies, 1967, p. xxxii), and the possibility of producing further confusion by incorrectly modernizing names which, in some cases, are no longer in use was a very real one. Only the most obvious misprints or slips of the pen have therefore been altered amongst the minor names. For the parishes, the forms given in Davies have been adopted, alternative or ancient spellings being included in brackets where possible difficulties might arise for the user. Where different English and Welsh forms exist, the parish has been listed under its English form, the Welsh form being given for reference, but the Welsh conventional alphabetical order has been adopted, so that 'd' precedes 'dd', 'l' precedes 'll', 'f' precedes 'll', and 'r' precedes 'rh'.

ACT AND AWARD DATES

As has already been mentioned, Wales escapes the problems created by the 1836 Act, since there were no enclosures under this legislation. All enclosures prior to 1845 therefore have an individual Act, and the date given refers to this. Any amending Acts are recorded under the original. Most of the Acts concerned were classified as 'Local and Personal' from 1800 to 1814, and it may be assumed that they fall into this category unless otherwise specified, and that they were officially 'Printed'. Those 'Not Printed' are specifically recorded as such in the listings, for they were numbered separately and in the British Library collection they are to be found bound with the Private Acts. It should be noted that some Acts were privately printed, and printed copies may exist in spite of their official 'Not Printed' designation. Where Acts fall under any other heading this has also been specifically recorded.

Under the different procedures from 1845 onwards, individual Acts were not normally necessary: the enclosure was usually set in motion by a Provisional Order, which was then confirmed in a general Act covering several enclosures. This confirmed order was the equivalent authority to the private Acts of the earlier period, and it is this date which is given prominence in the listings, the other details following.

As for the award date, this is normally straightforward, assuming that one can be traced. Where several awards followed from a single Act, one of two forms has been adopted according to the circumstances. If the awards are all separate, dealing with different parts of the land specified to be enclosed, the dates of all are included at the head; where they merely amended some detail of the original award, they are recorded amongst the further details.

NATIONAL GRID REFERENCE

For the National Grid references both letters and numbers have been given for the 100 kilometre square, followed by the six figure location within it. The Ordnance Survey now indicates the 100 kilometre squares by letters in their keys, but continues to give the numbers in the margins of the 1:50,000 topographic series, and it is these numbers, rather than the letters, which appear on the older map series where researchers may need to look for evidence of the areas concerned. Normally the reference is to the village or hamlet with which the lands enclosed were associated, but it must be appreciated that in a few cases the lands were both fragmented and spread over a very large area, and the reference can give only a rough indication of where they were located. Where the lands were known to lie in a compact block at a considerable distance from the place from which the enclosure takes its name, a reference to a point as near as possible to the centre of the lands has been given.

TYPE OF LAND AND AREA

While the type of land and the area affected by any enclosure are of fundamental importance, precise information on these points is not always easy to come by. Not all Acts or awards provide this information, and where they do it certainly cannot be relied upon (Chapman, 1978, and Chapman and Harris, 1982). The description of the land was sometimes reduced to a series of formal standard phrases, and the areas given by either Act or award can be wildly inaccurate in extreme cases. Furthermore, it is not clear precisely what the acreages are intended to include: the land affected by enclosure might be substantially greater than the amount of open or common land, since varying quantities of already-enclosed land were often redistributed by the award, and award totals, at least, may well include this, while Act totals are unlikely to do so.

In these circumstances, the Act and award figures given in the listings must be treated with caution. They are recorded exactly as given (rounded to the nearest whole acre), and though they are usually a fair indication of the order of size involved, they should not be accepted as having any greater precision than that. Many may in fact be much more accurate, especially those taken from the Orders and the awards associated with them, but there is no ready means of determining which are the inaccurate ones other than by totalling each individual allotment. Where this has been done, this total is given as 'Actual', and refers to all land affected by the award, including exchanges of old enclosed land, but usually excluding land taken for roads, for which the area is only rarely given in the award.

COMMISSIONERS OR VALUERS

In most cases this information is straightforward. The commissioner, or sometimes a team of commissioners, is named in the Act and in the award. In the event of his death or incapacity, he was replaced, and the changes are given in the award. Under the 1845 Act, the commissioner's approximate equivalent was designated a 'valuer', and details appear only in the award. Occasionally no commissioner was necessary, as, for example, when the Act contained the terms of the award (e.g. 48005, Caernarfon), and this is recorded in the listings. Problems arise only where the award is missing, since it is possible that the original commissioners failed to complete the work, as at Penmorfa (48013). In cases such as these, the listings name those given in the original Act, plus any changes discovered from other sources. Where two commissioners were appointed, an arbitrator was often appointed in addition, to adjudicate in the event of any disagreement between them. These arbitrators have also been recorded, though in many cases they were not required to act. Where the Crown had a direct interest in an enclosure it was common practice to appoint an assistant commissioner, with the specific brief of safeguarding that interest, and these too have been listed. On the other hand, the permanent 'Inclosure Commissioners', whose role was to confirm the valuer's award, and whose names may be encountered in some later awards, have been omitted.

The problem of identifying the surveyors has been alluded to already, but they have been included where this is possible without extensive searches of secondary documents. The other officials were only rarely referred to in the formal record, and they have been omitted even for the handful of enclosures where their names are known.

AWARDS

The aim of this section is to enable researchers to locate existing copies of the award, or awards. Copies of the maps and plans which exist detached from the awards have also been recorded, though it must be noted that, on their own, the value of some of these to the researcher is very limited. Minor abstracts and extracts have not been noted unless the whole award is missing and these are therefore a significant source of evidence.

The varying forms of words used to indicate that no extant copy of the award is known reflects the degree of certainty that one was, or was not, made in the first place. It is of course virtually impossible to be absolutely certain that one was never made, and it is quite possible that previously unknown examples may yet appear from private collections. However, there are some enclosures where I have been unable to find any evidence that the process was even started, while at the opposite extreme there are those where a copy is known to have existed but has subsequently vanished. Between the two extremes are a range of cases where it can be shown that the process began, but not that it was ever completed. While such a failure to complete may seem curious at first sight, there were various reasons why this might have happened. For example, it is likely that some landowners were able to come to a private agreement after the passing of the Act, and were thus able to avoid the heavy costs of a formal award by the commissioners. This may perhaps be the case for Welshpool (56019), where a later agreement to enclose appears to refer to lands specified in an uncompleted Act. It is also possible that the proprietors lost interest, either because changing economic circumstances made an enclosure no longer attractive or because the initial survey and valuation work showed that their assessments of the potential profits had been highly optimistic. There is therefore no reason to assume that because an Act was passed there must once have been an award as well.

PRINCIPAL ALLOTTEES

The listing of the principal allottees presented a number of problems. Though the commissioners obviously had to record to whom each plot was allotted, they were under no obligation to provide any summary or grand total for each individual, nor were they forced to present the material in any particular logical order. Thus while some awards do specify the totals granted to each individual, and some even provide a tabulated summary, others merely record the details of each plot. Where the number of plots is small, and the award is drawn up by owner, often alphabetically, these totals can be readily determined.

However, the number of plots may run into many hundreds, and so, even, can the number of owners. Furthermore, some awards adopt a quite different logic to listing by owner. Many Welsh awards list each township separately, owners appearing several times in different parts of the award if they had established claims in several townships, as was frequently the case. In a few enclosures, awards for different townships were actually physically separated and presented as discrete awards, though legally they formed part of a single entity. The complexities are increased where there was an active market in the land, for not only may an owner appear many times, but his purchased plots may appear in the alphabetical order of the original owner, even though it is the new owner's name which is recorded. Finally, and most confusing of all, there are a substantial number of awards where whatever logic was used is no longer apparent, and the allotments to any individual seem to be scattered randomly through the document. Though it is perfectly possible to disentangle the ownership patterns, this would have involved a time commitment far in excess of that available for the compilation of this guide. The detail given under this heading therefore varies from a precise statement of the principal allottees, together with the area of their allotments, to a mere list of the names of those who are mentioned in the Act. Great care is necessary with the latter, for it was normal practice in Wales to list people according to their social status rather than to their claims on the land concerned. Anyone who was not at least 'Esquire' was unlikely to be mentioned, even though he might be a major owner, while some of those mentioned might have had only minimal claims. Both the King himself and various powerful and wealthy landowners received minute fragments of land at some enclosures (e.g. Shirenewton, 55009); conversely, two farmers, for example, each received over 33 per cent of the land at the enclosure of St David's (57010).

Where precise figures are available, the vast differences in the amounts of land involved makes consistency between awards undesirable. An allottee who received almost the whole of the land distributed by one of the smaller enclosures would have an acreage which would not merit a mention in one of the larger ones, and the percentages of land allocated to individuals varies equally wildly, so that a common figure of, say, ten per cent of the total might produce as many as nine principal allottees in one and none at all in another. In these circumstances the definition of 'principal' has had to be an arbitrary and variable one, adapted as realistically as possible to the circumstances of each individual entry. A figure of ten per cent or of 100 acres has been adopted as the norm. Allotment totals have been rounded to the nearest whole acre, except in one or two cases where such rounding would have produced an anomalous result, for example, by appearing to remove an allottee below the ten per cent limit.

PAPERS

This was intended to draw the reader's attention to minute books, letters, and other such records known to exist for a particular enclosure. It is in no way comprehensive, for many documents of this type may well exist in private hands. For late nineteenth-century enclosures there are usually papers in the MAF collection of the Public Record Office, and specific attention has been drawn to these only where they are of special significance.

NOTES

The main aim of this section is to provide a source of cross-references to other works. In particular, the reference number given to the Act in Jeffreys Jones's standard work on Welsh Acts of Parliament is recorded, to permit easy cross-checking. Discrepancies between this list and those of Bowen and Dodd are also noted. This section has also been used for any explanatory material which may prove helpful to the user.

COUNTY SUMMARIES

In calculating the totals enclosed for each county a distinction has been made between those enclosures where some specific figure is recorded in one or other of the documents (listed as 'Recorded') and those where my own estimates have had to be used (listed as 'Estimated'). From what has already been said, it will be appreciated that even the 'Recorded' figures are not necessarily highly accurate. Where several figures are available, 'Actual' figures have been used in preference to 'award' ones, and 'award' in preference to 'Act'. In a few cases figures given in the Board of Agriculture Reports have been used in preference to the Act ones, since the authors almost certainly had access to detailed information. For example, Charles Hassall, author of the Monmouthshire and of the provisional Pembrokeshire Reports, was a commissioner on several of the awards.
My own estimates have been based, where possible, on inspection of the enclosure maps. Where this was not possible, an estimate has been made by attempting to identify the areas concerned on other maps. Such estimates inevitably lack precision, but it is hoped that they are at least of the correct order of magnitude. Certainly, the figures given here represent a more accurate assessment

than that produced some years ago, when the estimates from a sample of very small total size were inflated by the inclusion of the enormous Brecknock Forest award (Chapman, 1987).

THE DIRECTORY OF WELSH ENCLOSURE COMMISSIONERS

This is intended to provide a reference list, and to give some indication of the scope of each individual's activities. Where possible, birth and death dates are recorded, together with the period during which he was active on enclosure work. The figures for enclosures refer to activities as commissioner or valuer, unless otherwise specified; those for England are not necessarily a complete record, but have been given to indicate that some of those involved were active outside Wales. By convention, all commissioners tended to be referred to as 'gentleman', and status or occupation has been given only when some alternative was recorded. In later years many were in fact professional surveyors or land agents, and valuers under the 1845 legislation were usually called 'land surveyor' in the documents.

References

CHAPMAN, J. (1972) 'Agriculture and the "Waste" in Monmouthshire from 1750 to the Present Day' (Unpublished PhD thesis, University of London).
CHAPMAN, J. (1976) 'Parliamentary Enclosure in the Uplands: the case of the North York Moors', *Agricultural History Review*, 24, 337-341.
CHAPMAN, J. (1978) 'Some Problems in the Interpretation of Enclosure Awards', *Agricultural History Review*, 26, 108-114.
CHAPMAN, J. (1980) 'The Parliamentary Enclosures of West Sussex', *Southern History*, 2, 73-91.
CHAPMAN, J. (1982) 'The Unofficial Enclosure Proceedings: a study of the Horsham (Sussex) enclosure, 1812-13', *Sussex Archaeological Collections*, 120, 185-191.
CHAPMAN, J. (1987) 'The Extent and Nature of Parliamentary Enclosure' *Agricultural History Review*, 35, 25-35.
CHAPMAN, J. and HARRIS, T.M. (1982) 'The Accuracy of Enclosure Estimates: some evidence from Northern England', *Journal of Historical Geography*, 8, 261-264.
DAVIES, E. (1967). *A Gazetteer of Welsh Place-Names*. 3rd edition (Cardiff: University of Wales Press).
EDWARDS, J.W. (1963) 'Enclosure and agricultural improvement in the Vale of Clwyd, 1750-1875' (Unpublished M.A. Thesis, University of London).
HASSALL, C. (1812) *A General View of the Agriculture of the County of Monmouth* (London).

RODGERS, W.S. (1962) 'West Riding Commissioners of Enclosure, 1729-1850', *Yorkshire Archaeological Journal*, 40, 401-19.
SLATER, G. (1896) *The English peasantry and the enclosure of the common fields* (London).
TURNER, M.E.(ed.) (1978) *A Domesday of English enclosure acts and awards by W.E.Tate* (Reading).

ABBREVIATIONS

The following abbreviations have been used in the listings:

BoA Board of Agriculture Reports. For full titles see Davies (1815) and Hassall (1812) in the Bibliography.

CRO County Record Office. This refers to the office or suboffice located in the *historic* county concerned, unless otherwise indicated. For Denbighshire records held at Hawarden are listed as CROH, and for Flint those at Ruthin as CROR.

JJ Reference number to act, as given in Jeffreys Jones. (see bibliography)

NLW National Library of Wales, Aberystwyth.

PRO(Chancery) Public Record Office, Chancery Lane Branch, London

PRO(Kew) Public Record Office, Kew Branch, London.

All references are included in the Bibliography of Welsh Enclosures except:-

Eden P. *Dictionary of Land Surveyors 1580-1850*, Folkestone, 1975-9.

Slater's *Royal National and Commercial Directory and Topography of the Counties of ... Monmouthshire .... and South Wales*, London, 1851.

COUNTY SUMMARIES

COUNTY	AWARDS	ACREAGE
ANGLESEY		
All recorded	8	6,765
BRECONSHIRE		
All recorded	20	43,835
CAERNARFONSHIRE		
Recorded	10	38,870
Estimated	3	17,010
CARDIGANSHIRE		
All recorded	15	45,252
CARMARTHENSHIRE		
Recorded	26	24,102
Estimated	2	5,300
DENBIGHSHIRE		
Recorded	20	71,488
Estimated	4	26,000
FLINT		
All recorded	22	33,535
GLAMORGAN		
Recorded	10	7,798
Estimated	3	40
MERIONETHSHIRE		
All recorded	8	48,805
MONMOUTHSHIRE		
All recorded	13	14,677
MONTGOMERYSHIRE		
Recorded	18	60,878
Estimated	1	20,000
PEMBROKESHIRE		
All recorded	10	9,166
RADNORSHIRE		
All recorded	34	52,359
TOTAL WALES		
Recorded	214	457,530
Estimated	13	68,350
GRAND TOTAL	227	525,880

ANGLESEY

BODAFON   See Penrhosllugwy (46001).

CERRIGCEINWEN   See Llangefni (46006).

46002   HOLYHEAD (CAERGYBI)

Order 1859. Award 1861.
Provisional Order of 21 April 1859, confirmed by 22-23 Vic. c. 47.

Grid reference: SH (23) 247 827.

Common and waste: 20 acres (order and actual).

Cuttir Bodwredd and Cuttir Ty Mawr.

Valuer: William Dew of Bangor.
Assistant Commissioner: J. S. Rawlinson.

Award: i)   PRO (Kew) MAF 1/815; ii)   PRO (Chancery) LRRO 1/3007;   iii) CRO W/Maps/12.

Principal allottees: The Hon. William Owen Stanley received 17 acres.

Notes: JJ 2364.

46008   LLANBEDR-GOCH (LLANBEDRGOCH)

Order 1860. Award 1864.
Provisional Order of 28 July 1859, confirmed by 23-24 Vic. c. 17.

Grid reference: SH (23) 520 794.

Common and waste: 69 acres (award), 68 acres (actual).

Rhos-y-Gad Common, apparently lying in Llanbedr-goch, sometimes listed as a hamlet in Llanfair Mathafarn Eithaf. Originally listed as in Llanfair Pwllgwyngyll parish.

Valuer: Robert Algeo of Hendy in Llanfair Pwllgwyngyll.

Award: PRO (Kew) MAF 1/970.

Principal allottees: Two exceeded 10 per cent – Colonel Thomas Peers Williams (25 acres) and the Marquis of Anglesey (20 acres).

Notes: JJ 2366.

LLANDYSILIO   See Llaneilian (46003).

LLANDDYFNAN   See Llangefni (46006).

46003   LLANEILIAN

Act   54 Geo. III c. 161 1814.   Awards 1821, 1827.

Grid reference: SH (23) 470 929.

Common and waste: 290 acres (Act).

Llaneilian Marsh. Recorded as partly also in Llandysilio parish.

Commissioner: Walter Jones of Cefn Rug in Corwen, who died and was replaced by Richard Yates of Gravel Hill, Montgomery. Yates had been the surveyor.

Award: i)   CRO W/Maps 7 and 22;   ii) PRO (Chancery) LRRO 1/3027 and 1/3028 (plans).

Principal allottees: Act records Bishop of Bangor, Earl of Uxbridge, Lord Boston, Sir John Williams, Sir John S. Stanley, Revd Edward Hughes, Owen Williams, and John Price.

Notes: JJ 2307.

LLANFAIR MATHAFARN EITHAF   See Llanbedr-goch (46008).

LLANFAIR PWLLGWYNGYLL   See Llanbedr-goch (46008).

46004   LLANFECHELL

Order 1862.   Award 1869.
Provisional Order of 14 November 1861, confirmed by 25-26 Vic. c. 47.

Grid reference: SH (23) 369 913.

Common and waste: 248 acres (award), 254 acres (actual).

Llanfechell Mountain.

Valuer: Thomas Jones of Denbigh, who died and was replaced by Richard Wakeford Attree of Ruabon, who in turn resigned and was replaced by Abraham Foulkes of Ruabon. Attree's address is given as Westminster, but he apparently lived in Ruabon. He resigned following objections to his original award.

Award: i)   PRO (Kew) MAF 1/750;   ii)   NLW WCC Deposit Shelf 48;   iii) PRO (Chancery) LRRO 1/3024 (plan).

Principal allottees: Two exceeded 10 per cent – William Bulkeley Hughes (120 acres) and Captain James King (27 acres).

Notes: JJ 2369.

46005   LLANFIHANGEL ESGEIFIOG (LLANFIHANGEL YSCEIFIOG)

Act   51 Geo. III c. 132 1811.   Award 1821.

Grid reference: SH (23) 478 735.

Common and waste: 2747 acres (award), 2551 acres (from reference table).

Malltraeth and Cors Ddyga Marshes. Partly also in parishes of Llanidan, Llangaffo, Llangristiolus and Trefdraeth.

Commissioners: Original Act of 1788 appointed Evan Lloyd of Maesyporth; Revd Richard Griffith of Bangor; Revd John Williams of Treffos. Lloyd and Griffith both died, and the 1811 Act added John Williams of Tregarnedd and Benjamin Wyatt of Lime Grove. The latter died in 1818, and was replaced by James Wyatt, also of Lime Grove.

Award: i) Formerly in the hands of local solicitor. Present whereabouts unknown; ii) Copy of plan in PRO (Chancery) LRRO 1/3019, with reference table.

Principal allottees: Four exceeded 200 acres – William Lewis Hughes (762 acres), Owen Pulland Meyrick (245 acres), Holland Griffith (244 acres), and the Marquis of Anglesey (242 acres).

Papers: i) PRO (Chancery) CREST 6/108 and 6/145.
ii) CRO (Caernarfon) X/Poole/1727-1768.

Notes: JJ 2279, 2219, and 2223. The enclosure was originally begun under Acts of 1788, 28 Geo. III c. 71 (Public), and 1790, 30 Geo. III c. 59 (Public), but abandoned. Bowen also lists Act of 1754-5, apparently in error. Act later amended by 22-23 Vic. c. 108 (L and P), 1859 (JJ 2365).

LLANFIHANGEL TRE'R-BEIRDD See Penrhosllugwy (46001).

LLANGAFFO See Llanfihangel Esgeifiog (46005).

46006 LLANGEFNI

Act 52 Geo III c. 169 1812. Award 1814.

Grid reference: SH (23) 458 759.

Common and waste: 1200 acres (Act).

Rhos y meirch, Talwrn mawr, Mynydd Llanddyfnan, Mynydd Llwydiart, Pentraeth Marsh. Partly in parishes of Cerrigceinwen, Llanddyfnan and Pentraeth.

Commissioner: John Maughan of Barnt Green, Worcestershire.
Assistant Commissioner: Edward Griffith Roberts of Caernarfon.

Award: i) Formerly with local solicitor. Present whereabouts unknown; ii) PRO (Chancery) LRRO 1/3018 (apparently draft plans).

Principal allottees: The draft plans indicate Paul Panton, the King, Owen Puttland Meyrick, Lord Bulkeley, and the Misses Lewis as the major allottees.

Notes: JJ 2292.

LLANGEINWEN See Newborough (46007).

LLANGRISTIOLUS See Llanfihangel Esgeifiog (46005).

LLANIDAN See Llanfihangel Esgeifiog (46005).

46007 NEWBOROUGH (NIWBWRCH)

Act 55 Geo. III c. 37 1815. Award 1843.

Grid reference: SH (23) 435 656.

Common and waste: 2300 acres (Act).

Partly in Llangeinwen.

Commissioner: John Maughan of Luton and later of Barnt Green, Worcestershire.
Surveyor: Richard Yates of Gravel Hill, Montgomery.

Award: i) CRO (Caernarfon) INC AW 16; ii) PRO (Chancery) LRRO 1/3021 (plan); iii) CRO W/Maps/5.

Principal allottees: Act records the King, Thomas Wyatt, Borough of Newborough and others.

Notes: JJ 2314.

46001 PENRHOSLLUGWY (RHOS LLIGWY)

Order 1866. Award 1870.
Provisional Order of 4 January 1866, confirmed by 29-30 Vic. c. 94.

Grid reference: SH (23) 470 850.

Common and waste: 82 acres (order).

Mynydd Bodafon. Partly in Llanfihangel Tre'r-beirdd.

Valuer: Robert Algeo of Menai Bridge.

Award: i) PRO (Kew) MAF 1/1058; ii) CRO W/Maps/12; iii) PRO (Chancery) LRRO 1/3026.

Principal allottees: Almost all land sold to cover expenses. John Lewis Hampton Lewis was the only allottee to receive over 10 acres, having purchased 64 acres.

Notes: JJ 2379.

PENTRAETH   See Llangefni (46006).

RHOS-Y-GAD See Llanbedr-goch (46008).

TREFDRAETH See Llanfihangel Esgeifiog (46005).

TWYN TREWAN (TOWYN TREWAN)

Awards of 1910 and 1911 in PRO (Kew) MAF 1/1089 and 1/184. Apparently a Regulation only, and therefore excluded from consideration here.

BRECONSHIRE

ALEXANDERSTONE   See Llan-ddew (47008).

ALLT-MAWR   See Llanddewi'r-cwm (47007).

47001   BATTLE (Y BATEL)

Order 1860. Award 1862.
Provisional Order of 22 December 1859, confirmed by 23-24 Vic. c. 17.

Grid reference: SO (32) 010 310.

Common and waste: 383 acres (award), 406 acres (actual).

Battle Common.

Valuer: Isaac Davies of Brecon.

Award: i)   PRO (Kew) MAF 1/650;   ii)   NLW Brecon Q/RA/10.

Principal allottees: Colonel John Lloyd Vaughan Watkins received 84 per cent (241 acres).

Papers: Brecknock Museum.

Notes: JJ 2366. Award amended 1868.

47002   BRECKNOCK FOREST (FFOREST FAWR)

Act 48 Geo. III c. 73 (Public General) 1808. Award 1819.

Grid reference: SN (22) 900 180.

Common and waste: 40,000 acres (award), 39,510 acres (actual).

Commissioners: Henry De Bruyn of London; John Cheese (senior) of Lyonshall, Herefordshire.
Surveyors: Samuel Wharton; David Davies.

Award: i) PRO (Chancery) E 159/711 rot. 40 and 41, and MR 132;   ii) CRO B/QS/DE/1.

Principal allottees: Largest area left open and common (17,646 acres). The King received 13,860 acres, and the tithe owner 292 acres. Much land was sold, the major buyers being William Rowland Alder (4304 acres) and Archibald Christie (1787 acres).

Notes: JJ 2253, 2313, and 2321. He also gives (under 2228) 34 Geo. III c. 75, but the award refers to the 1808 Act as the authority. The Acts of 1815 and 1818 involved minor amendments. The area is often refered to as The Great Forest of Brecknock.

47003 BRONLLYS (BRWYNLLYS)

Order 1860. Award 1863.
Provisional Order of 22 December 1859, confirmed by 23-24 Vic. c. 17.

Grid reference: SO (32) 144 350.

Common fields: 105 acres (order), 106 acres (actual), excluding old enclosures.

Valuer: Isaac Davies of Brecon.

Award: i)   PRO (Kew) MAF 1/1/334;   ii)   NLW Brecon Q/RA/4

Principal allottees: Three exceeded 10 per cent - the Earl of Ashburnham (31 acres), Mrs Anna Holford and John W. Roche (18 acres), and William L. Banks (12 acres).

Papers: Brecknock Museum.

Notes: JJ 2366.

47015 CANTREF (CANTRIFF)

Order 1856. Award 1858.
Provisional Order of 19 March 1856, confirmed by 19-20 Vic. c. 106.

Grid reference: SO (32) 010 185.

Common and waste: 20 acres (award and actual).

Mynyddfirnach Common.

Valuer: Isaac Davies of Brecon.

Award: i)   PRO (Kew) MAF 1/891;   ii)   NLW Brecon Q/RA/9.

Principal allottees: Two exceeded 20 per cent – Revd Richard W. P. Davies (7 acres) and William Pearce (7 acres).

Papers: Brecknock Museum.

Notes: JJ 2359. Award amended 1870.

47004   CATHEDIN (CATHEDINE)

Order 1859. Award 1861.
Provisional Order of 3 June 1858, confirmed by 22 Vic. c. 3.

Grid reference: SO (32) 143 252.

Common and waste: 528 acres (award), 526 acres (actual).

Cathedine Common.

Valuer: Isaac Davies of Brecon.

Award: PRO (Kew) MAF 1/282.

Principal allottees: Only one exceeded 10 per cent, James P. W. G. Holford (407 acres).

Papers: Brecknock Museum.

Notes: JJ 2363.

CEFN ARTHEN   See Llywel (47005). NLW says Traean Mawr parish.

CILWYCH   See Llanfihangel Cwmdu (47018).

GARTHBRENGI

47006   (i) Order 1861. Award 1865.
Provisional Order of 29 November 1860, confirmed by 24-25 Vic. c. 38.

Grid reference: SO (32) 045 336.

Common and waste: 110 acres (award), 109 acres (actual).

Garthbrengy Common.

Valuer: Isaac Davies of Brecon.

Award: i)   PRO (Kew) MAF 1/774;   ii)   NLW Brecon Q/RA/2.

Principal allottees: Three exceeded 20 acres – John Dilwyn Llewelyn (40 acres), Baron Tredegar (24 acres), and Revd Thomas Watkins (23 acres).

Papers: Brecknock Museum.

Notes: JJ 2368.

47020 (ii) Order 1861. Award 1865.
Provisional Order of 29 November 1860, confirmed by 24-25 Vic. c. 38.

Grid reference: SO (32) 060 335.

Common and waste: 144 acres (award and actual).

Talwen Common.

Valuer: Isaac Davies of Brecon.

Award: i)   PRO (Kew) MAF 1/772;   ii)   NLW Brecon Q/RA/11.

Principal allottees: Four exceeded 10 per cent – John I. W. Fredricks (50 acres), Sir Charles M Robinson (27 acres), John Jones (22 acres), and David Watkins Lloyd (22 acres).

Papers: Brecknock Museum.

Notes: JJ 2368.

HENALLT   See Llanddewi'r-Cwm (47007).

LLANDYFAELOG FACH (LLANDEFAELOG)

47019 (i) Order 1860. Award 1862.
Provisional Order of 22 December 1859, confirmed by 23-24 Vic. c. 55.

Grid reference: SO (32) 028 328.

Common and waste: 228 acres (award), 212 acres (actual).

Sarnau Common.

Valuer: Isaac Davies of Brecon.

Award: i) PRO (Kew) MAF 1/331; ii) NLW Brecon Q/RA/13.

Principal allottees: Three exceeded 10 per cent – the Marquis of Camden (62 acres), Colonel John Lloyd Watkins (40 acres), and Revd Walter Jones (23 acres).

Papers: Brecknock Museum.

Notes: JJ 2367.

(ii) See Llanfihangel Fechan (47010).

LLAN-DDEW (LLANTHEW)

47008 (i) Act 54 Geo. III c. 2 (not printed) 1813. Award ?.

Grid reference: SO (32) 072 301.

Common and waste: 195 acres (Act).

Allt yr Onon (Onnen), Wain Gyfir, in manors of Alexanderstone and Mara Mota.

Commissioner: William Couling of Brecon (from Act).

Award: Not known.

Principal allottees: Act names only the Lord, Sir Charles Morgan.

Notes: JJ 2308.

47009 (ii) Order 1860. Award 1865.
Provisional Order of 29 November 1860, confirmed by 24-25 Vic. c. 38.

Grid reference: SO (32) 055 308.

Common and waste: 72 acres (order), 74 acres (actual).

Llan-ddew Common in Brecon manor.

Valuer: Isaac Davies of Brecon.

Award: i) PRO (Kew) MAF 1/967; ii) NLW Brecon Q/RA/7.

Principal allottees: Two exceeded 10 per cent – Colonel John Lloyd Watkins (23 acres) and Thomas Cummins (22 acres).

Papers: Brecknock Museum.

Notes: JJ 2368.

47007 LLANDDEWI'R-CWM

Order 1855. Award 1857.
Provisional Order of 23 June 1855, confirmed by 18-19 Vic. c. 61.

Grid reference: SO (32) 050 475.

Common and waste: 108 acres (award), 106 acres (actual).

Henallt Common. Partly in Allt-mawr.

Valuer: Isaac Davies of Brecon.

Award: i) PRO (Kew) MAF 1/878; ii) NLW Brecon Q/RA/16.

Principal allottees: Three exceeded 10 per cent – Sir Joseph Bailey (71 acres), Thomas Price Bligh (21 acres), and William Powell (14 acres).

Papers: Brecknock Museum.

Notes: JJ 2356.

47018 LLANFIHANGEL CWM DU (ST MICHAELS)

Order 1855. Award 1857.
Provisional Order of 19 April 1855, confirmed by 18-19 Vic. c. 61.

Grid reference: SO (32) 172 205.

Common and waste: 244 acres (award and actual).

Myarth Hill, in hamlets of Tretŵr (Tretower) and Cilwych.

Valuer: Isaac Davies of Brecon.

Award: i) PRO (Kew) MAF 1/791; ii) NLW Brecon Q/RA/5.

Principal allottees: Sir Joseph Bailey received 223 acres.

Papers: Brecknock Museum.

Notes: JJ 2356.

47010   LLANFIHANGEL FECHAN

Order 1861. Award 1865.
Provisional Order of 29 November 1860, confirmed by 24-25 Vic. c. 38.

Grid reference: SO (32) 028 357.

Common and waste: 720 acres (order and actual).

Land in Brecon manor. At the time of enclosure, Llanfihangel was recorded as a hamlet in Llandyfaelog parish.

Valuer: Isaac Davies of Brecon.

Award: i)   PRO (Kew) MAF 1/226 and /958;   ii)   NLW Brecon Q/RA/14.

Principal allottees: Four received over 10 per cent – Hugh Powell Price (313 acres), the Bridgewater family (118 acres), the Marquis of Camden (111 acres), and Revd Thomas Watkins (80 acres).

Papers: Brecknock Museum.

Notes: JJ 2368.

LLANFILO (LLANFILLO)   See Llansanffraid (47012).

47011   LLANGANTEN

Order 1855. Award 1857.
Provisional Order of 19 June 1855, confirmed by 18-19 Vic. c. 61.

Grid reference: SN (22) 990 519.

Common and waste: 26 acres (order and actual).

Rhydins Common.

Valuer: Isaac Davies of Brecon.

Award: i) PRO (Kew) MAF 1/879, ii) NLW Brecon Q/RA/3.

Principal allottees: Sir Joseph Bailey and Thomas Price Bligh split the land almost equally (12 and 14 acres respectively).

Papers: Brecknock Museum.

Notes: JJ 2356.

47012 LLANSANFFRAID (LLANSAINTFFRAID)

Act 54 Geo. III c. 54 (not printed) 1814. Award 1817.

Grid reference: SO (32) 122 235.

Common and waste: No acreage given in Act, 466 acres (actual).

Various manors in Penkelly (Pencelli). Partly in Llanfilo parish.

Commissioners: David Davies of Llangattock; Thomas Morley of St Michael Cwmdu, and later of Llangynidr.

Award: NLW Brecon Q/RA/17.

Principal allottees: Two received over 10 per cent – Thyne Howe Gwynne senior (118 acres) and Walter Powell (83 acres).

Papers: PRO (Chancery) CREST 6/145.

Notes: JJ 2311.

LLYS-WEN

47013 (i) Order 1856. Award 1858.
Provisional Order of 19 March 1856, confirmed by 19-20 Vic. c. 106.

Grid reference: SO (32) 134 380.

Common: 31 acres (order and actual).

Llyswen Common.

Valuer: Isaac Davies of Brecon.

Award: i)   PRO (Kew) MAF 1/890;   ii)   NLW Brecon Q/RA/6.

Principal allottees: Two received over 20 per cent – Sir Charles Morgan R. Morgan (15 acres) and Sir Joseph Bailey (7 acres).

Papers: Brecknock Museum.

Notes: JJ 2359. Award of 5 March.

47014 (ii) Order 1856. Award 1858.
Provisional Order of 19 March, confirmed by 19-20 Vic. c. 106.

Grid reference: SO (32) 134 380.

Open field: 50 acres (order), 50 acres (actual, excluding lands exchanged).

Llyswen Fields.

Valuer: Isaac Davies of Brecon.

Award: i)   PRO (Kew) MAF 1/893;   ii)   NLW Brecon Q/RA/12.

Principal allottees: Baron Tredegar received 33 acres.

Papers: Brecknock Museum.

Notes: JJ 2359. Award of 22 April. Though the date of the order is identical to 47013, these were technically completely independent enclosures.

47005 LLYWEL

Order 1849. Award 1857.
Provisional Order of 29 January 1849, confirmed by 12-13 Vic. c. 7.

Grid reference: SN (22) 870 300.

Common and waste: 316 acres (order), 316 acres (actual, excluding 13 acres exchanged).

Cefn Arthen (Erthan) Common, in hamlet of Traian Mawr (Traean-mawr).

Valuer: Thomas Saunders of Lampeter Pont Stephen.

Award: i)   PRO (Kew) MAF 1/788;   ii)   NLW Brecon Q/RA/1.

Principal allottees: The Marquis of Camden received 269 acres.

Notes: JJ 2346. Sometimes wrongly listed as Traian Manor.

MARA MOTA   See Llan-ddew (47008).

47016   MERTHYR CYNOG

Order 1861. Award 1865.
Provisional Order of 29 November 1860, confirmed by 24-25 Vic. c. 38.

Grid reference: SN (22) 984 375.

Common and waste: 450 acres (order), 449 acres (actual).

Mynydd Bach, Gaerfach, Carnole, Cwmllechach, and Cefn Gwar y Felin.

Valuer: Isaac Davies of Brecon.

Award: i)   PRO (Kew) MAF 1/771;   ii)   NLW Brecon Q/RA/15.

Principal allottees: Two received over 10 per cent – Hugh Powell Price (137 acres) and the Marquis of Camden (136 acres).

Papers: Brecknock Museum.

Notes: JJ not given.

MYARTH   See Llanfihangel Cwm Du (47018).

MYNYDDFIRNACH   See Cantref (47015).

RHYDINS   See Llanganten (47011).

SARNAU   See Llandyfaelog Fach (47019).

47017   TALACH-DDU

    Order 1861.   Award 1865.
    Provisional Order of 25 April 1861, confirmed by
      24-25 Vic. c. 38.

    Grid reference: SO (32) 082 331.

    Common and waste: 126 acres (order), 125 acres
      (actual).

    Talach-ddu Common.

    Valuer: Isaac Davies of Brecon.

    Award: i)   PRO (Kew) MAF 1/770;   ii)   NLW Brecon
      Q/RA/8.

    Principal allottees: Two received over 20 acres -
      Revd Charles Griffiths (25 acres) and John James
      Williams (21 acres).

    Papers: Brecknock Museum.

    Notes: JJ 2368.

TALWEN   See Garthbrengi (47020).

CAERNARFONSHIRE

ABERDARON

48001 (i) Act 42 Geo. III c. 30 1802. Award 1814.

Grid reference: SH (23) 203 299.

Common and waste, 2000 acres (Act), 1379 acres (actual).

Rhoshirwaun. Partly in Bryncroes and Llanfaelrhys parishes.

Commissioner: Benjamin Wyatt of The Terrace, Caernarfon.

Award: i) CRO INC AW 13; ii) PRO (Chancery) LRRO 1/3235 (plan).

Principal allottees: Only one, Sir Robert Williams Vaughan, received over 10 per cent. Three others received over 100 acres, all partly as a result of extensive purchases. These were Richard Edwards (130 acres), Evan Jones (125 acres), and William Glynne Griffith (108 acres).

Notes: JJ 2239.

48002 (ii) Act 51 Geo. III c. 49 (not printed) 1811. Award 1812, 1861.

Grid reference: SH (23) 210 267.

Common and waste: 6000 acres (Act).

Morfa Mawr, Rhosgwfil, Morfa Abererch, Rhosfawr, Morfa Neugwl, Mynydol Cilan, Goss Llyferin, Mynydd-y-Graig, Rhiw Mountain, Pen-y-cil, Braichystyn. Also in parishes of Llanfaelrhys, Bryncroes, Llanengan, Deneio, Penrhos and Abererch.
This enclosure covered many widely scattered pieces of waste. It appears to have been completed in many separate parts.

Commissioner: Richard Ellis of Pwllheli.

Award: i) PRO (Kew) MR 119; ii) NLW RM C31. (Photostat copy, PB 7590-7595); iii) CRO microfilm copy.

Principal allottees: Act records the King, Bishop of Bangor, Borough of Pwllheli, and seven others by name.

Notes: JJ 2285.

ABER-ERCH   See Aberdaron (48002).

BRYNCROES
(i)   See Aberdaron (48001).

(ii)   See Aberdaron (48002).

48003   CAERHUN (CAERHYN)

Order 1850. Award 1858.
Provisional Order of 8 February 1849, confirmed by 13-14 Vic. c. 8.

Grid reference: SH (23) 730 698.

Common and waste: 5840 acres (award), 5841 acres (actual).

Caerhyn Common.

Valuer: Edward Edwards of Bron Erch in Aber-erch.

Award: i)   PRO (Kew) MAF 1/23;   ii)   PRO (Chancery) LRRO 1/60 and MR 854;   iii) CRO INC AW 1.

Principal allottees: Two exceeded 10 per cent - Sir Richard Bulkeley Williams Bulkeley (1460 acres) and Hugh Davies Griffith (1226 acres).

Notes: JJ 2348.

48005   CAERNARFON (CAERNARVON)

Act 1882. Award None.

Grid reference: SH (23) 480 626.

Common and waste: area not stated.

Caernarfon Borough, in parish of Llanbeblig.

Notes: JJ 2388. The Act was to permit the corporation to acquire Morfa Seiont Common to create a public park, and no award was necessary.

CARNGUWCH See Nefyn (48011).

CLYNNOG See Nefyn (48011).

DENEIO See Aberdaron (48002).

DOLBENMAEN

48013 (i) Act 52 Geo. III c. 76 (not printed) 1812. Award 1826.

Grid reference: SH (23) 548 406.

Common and waste: area not stated.

In townships of Dolbenmaen, Llanfihangel-y-Pennant, and Penmorfa.

Commissioner: Walter Jones of Cefn Rug in Corwen (from Act. Jones could not have completed this award, as he died in 1815). Dodd states completed by Thomas Roberts (of Brynselwrn).

Award: Present whereabouts unknown; PRO (Chancery) LRRO 1/87 (plan) and MR 802 pt 1 (plan), listed as enclosures, appear to be copies of tithe.

Principal allottees: Act records the King, Bishop of Bangor, Mary Jane Crosby, Sir Thomas Mostyn, William Alexander Madocks and Richard Richards.

Notes: JJ 2299.

(ii) See Traeth Mawr (48012).

EGLWYS-FACH See DENBIGHSHIRE.

48004 **EGLWYS-RHOS**

Act 6-7 Vic. c. 14 1843. Awards 1848, 1849 and amendment 1862.

Grid reference: SH (23) 804 807.

Common and waste: area not stated in Act.

Partly in parishes of Llandudno, Llangystennin, and Llandrillo-yn-Rhos. Parts lie in DENBIGHSHIRE.

Commissioner: Richard Yates of Whittington.
Assistant Commissioner: John Jones of Plas Issa, Corwen.
Surveyor: Richard Piercy.

Award: i)   CRO INC AW 2, 3, 4;   ii) PRO (Chancery) LRRO 1/3275 (plan), and 1/3276.

Principal allottees: Act records Bishop of Bangor, and eighteen others by name.

Papers: PRO (Chancery) CREST 6/179 C;   PRO (Kew) MAF 25/8/B4041.

Notes: JJ 2336. The amendment was a minor legal formality.

GWEDIR (GWYDYR)   See Llanrwst (51020), under DENBIGHSHIRE.

LLANAELHAEARN   See Nefyn (48011).

LLANBEBLIG
(i)   See Llanrug (48010).

(ii)   See Caernarfon (48005).

48008   LLANBEDROG

Act 48 Geo. III c. 71 (not printed) 1808. Award 1825.

Grid reference: SH (23) 329 316.

Common and waste: 4000 acres (Act)

Mynydd Mynytho, Rhosddu, Carn Fadryn. Also in parishes of Llanfihangel Bachellaeth, Llangian and Llaniestyn.

Commissioner: Walter Jones of Corwen, who died and was replaced by Richard Ellis of Pwllheli. Jones had also been assistant commissioner in succession to Griffith Thomas of Maentwrog, who had died in 1813. He in turn was replaced by Edward Griffith Roberts.

Award: i)   CRO INC AW 6;   ii) PRO (Chancery) LRRO 1/3300 (plans, with table).

Principal allottees: Act records the King, Bishop of Bangor, Lord Newborough, Sir Thomas Mostyn,

Thomas Parry Jones, Thomas Assheton Smith, and Richard Edwards by name.

Notes: JJ 2259.

48006 LLANBEDRYCENNIN

Order 1850. Award 1858.
Provisional Order of 8 February 1849, confirmed by 13-14 Vic. c. 8.

Grid reference: SH (23) 760 695.

Common and waste: 400 acres (order), 401 acres (actual).

Waun-y-Gaer.

Valuer: Edward Edwards of Bron Erch in Aber-erch.

Award: i) PRO (Kew) MAF 1/135; ii) PRO (Chancery) LRRO 1/39 and MR 77; iii) CRO INC AW 15.

Principal allottees: Three exceeded 10 per cent – Hugh Davies Griffith (77 acres), Sir Richard Bulkeley Williams Bulkeley (76 acres), and John Williams (48 acres).

Papers: PRO (Chancery) CREST 6/179.

Notes: JJ 2348.

LLANDRILLO-YN-RHOS See Eglwys-Rhos (48004).

LLANDUDNO See Eglwys-Rhos (48004).

48009 LLANDWROG

Act 46 Geo. III c. 73 1806. Award 1831.

Grid reference: SH (23) 452 561.

Common and waste: 2560 acres (Dodd).

Morfa Dinas Dinlle, Morfa Cwtta, Rhos Pengwern. Partly in parishes of Llanwnda and Llanfaglen.

Commissioner: Walter Jones of Corwen, who died and was replaced by Thomas Roberts of Brynselwrn.

Award: i) CRO INC AW 11;   ii) PRO (Chancery) LRRO 1/3272b (plan).

Principal allottees: Act records Sir Robert Williams, Bishop of Bangor, Revd Richard Ellis, Lord Newborough, Sir Henry Owen, and Thomas Assheton Smith.

Papers: PRO (Chancery) CREST 2/1576;   CRO X/Poole/1769-1773.

Notes: JJ 2248.

48007 LLANDDEINIOLEN

Act   46 Geo. III c. 29 1806. Award 1814.

Grid reference: SH (23) 546 659.

Common and waste: 3346 acres (award), 3331 acres (actual).

Commissioner: Walter Jones of Cefn Rug in Corwen. Surveyor: Thomas Roberts of Brynselwrn.

Award: i) CRO INC AW 7;   ii) PRO (Chancery) LRRO 1/3239 (plan).

Principal allottees: Thomas Assheton Smith received over 80 per cent (2695 acres). Lord Newborough (110 acres), Rice Thomas (118 acres), and Thomas Wright (137 acres) exceeded 100 acres, the last largely by purchase.

Notes: JJ 2245 and 2257. Act amended by 48 Geo III c 39 (not printed) 1808.

LLANENGAN   See Aberdaron (48002).

LLANFAELRHYS
  (i)   See Aberdaron (48001).

  (ii)   See Aberdaron (48002).

LLANFAGLAN   See Llandwrog (48009).

LLANFIHANGEL BACHELLAETH   See Llanbedrog (48008).

LLANFIHANGEL-Y-PENNANT   See Dolbenmaen (48013).

LLANGÏAN   See Llanbedrog (48008).

LLANGYSTENNIN See Eglwys Rhos (48004).

LLANIESTYN See Llanbedrog (48008).

LLANLLYFNI See Nefyn (48011).

48010 LLANRUG

Act 46 Geo. III c. 36 1806. Award 1816 and 1820.

Grid reference: SH (23) 534 635.

Common and waste: 2258 acres (from summary table).

1816 award covers Treflan, Rhosrug, Cefn Du and part of Waunfawr, lying partly in parish of Llanbeblig. 1820 award covers Waunfawr and Garneddwen.

Commissioner: Walter Jones of Corwen, who died and was replaced by Thomas Roberts of Brynselwrn.

Award: i) CRO INC AW 8 (1820 award only); ii) PRO (Chancery) LRRO 1/3240 (plan).

Principal allottees: Four exceeded 10 per cent (excluding purchases) - Thomas Assheton Smith (476 acres), Hugh Rowlands (456 acres), Lord Newborough (306 acres), and Susannah Williams (238 acres).

Notes: JJ 2246.

LLANWNDA See Llandwrog (48009).

LLYSFAEN In CAERNARFONSHIRE at enclosure, but transferred to DENBIGHSHIRE. See 51022.

48011 NEFYN (NEVIN)

Act 52 Geo. III c. 75 (not printed) 1812. Award 1821.

Grid reference: SH (23) 309 407.

Common and waste: 10,000 acres (Dodd).

Yr Eifl, Nevin Mountain, Clogwyn, Carngiwch Mountain, Rhos Commins, Bwlchmawr, Gyrncoch, Bwlch derwen and Ynys wyllt. Also in parishes of Pistyll, Carnguwch, Clynnog, Llanllyfni, and Llanaelhaearn.

Commissioners: Robert Williams of Ty Coch; Richard Ellis of Pwllheli.

Award: i) CRO INC AW 12; ii) PRO (Chancery) LRRO 1/3255, 1/3256, 1/3257 (plans), 1/3298, 1/3299.

Principal allottees: Act records King, Sir Robert Williams, Borough of Nevin, Thomas Assheton Smith, William Harvey, Richard Edwards, and David Ellis.

Papers: PRO (Chancery) CREST 6/145.

Notes: JJ 2298.

PENMORFA   See Dolbenmaen (48013).

PENRHOS   See Aberdaron (48002).

PISTYLL   See Nefyn (48011).

RHIW   See Aberdaron (48002).

48012   **TRAETH MAWR**

Act   47 Geo. III c. 36 1807. Award 1823.

Grid reference: SH (23) 585 395.

Common and waste: 2700-3500 acres (Dodd).

Traeth Mawr Sands. The award of 1823 was only partial, and the remainder was apparently never formally completed. The area lay in the parishes of Dolbenmaen, and Ynyscynhaearn, and in Llanfihangel-y-Traethau and Llanfrothen in MERIONETHSHIRE.

Commissioner: John Matthews of Pen-y-bont in Mold.

Award: i) CRO INC AW 12; ii) CRO (Merioneth) Z/QR/EN/1 (photocopy).

Principal allottees: Act records King as vesting the lands in William A. Madocks.

Notes: JJ 2249. The Act was amended in 1821 by 1-2 Geo. IV c. 115.

WAEN-Y-GAER   See Llanbedrycennin (48006).

YNYSCYNHAEARN   See Traeth Mawr (48012).

CARDIGANSHIRE

49001 BLAENPENNAL

Order 1851. Award 1864.
Provisional Order of 20 June 1850, confirmed by 14-15 Vic. c. 2.

Grid reference: SN (22) 625 660.

Common and waste: 1420 acres (order), 1419 acres (actual).

Mynydd Bach in township of Blaenpennal. Partly in parishes of Llanrhystud, Llanbadarn-Trefeglwys, Llansanffraid, Cilcennin, and Llanddewibrefi.

Valuer: John William Rees of Pencarreg in Llanilar.

Award: i) PRO (Kew) MAF 1/287; ii) NLW Card C C Deposit 11.

Principal allottees: Only one exceeded 10 per cent, David Davies (192 acres).

Notes: JJ 2350.

49002 CARDIGAN (ABERTEIFI)

Order 1854. Award 1855.
Provisional Order of 2 December 1853, confirmed by 17-18 Vic. c. 9.

Grid reference: SN (22) 178 460.

Common and waste: 176 acres (award), 206 acres (order and actual).

Cardigan Common and Netpool Bank.

Valuer: David Davies of Froodvale.

Award: i) PRO (Kew) MAF 1/472; ii) NLW Card C C Deposit 1.

Principal allottees: Two exceeded 10 per cent - the Borough of Cardigan (120 acres) and Revd Robert H. W. Miles (48 acres).

Notes: JJ 2354.

49003 CELLAN

Order 1851. Award 1856.
Provisional Order of 13 November 1850, confirmed by 14-15 Vic. c. 2.

Grid reference: SN (22) 614 498.

Common and waste: 1970 acres (order), 2029 acres (actual).

Cellan Mountain.

Valuer: David Davies of Conwil Cayo.

Award: i) PRO (Kew) MAF 1/264; ii) NLW Card C C Deposit 2.

Principal allottees: None received 10 per cent. Largest was Baron Carrington (202 acres).

Notes: JJ 2350.

CEULAN-Y-MAES-MAWR   See Llangynfelyn (49008).

CILCENNIN
(i)   See Llanrhystud (49014).

(ii) See Blaenpennal (49001).

GWNNWS

49004 (i) Act 55 Geo. III c. 81 (not printed) 1815. Award ?

Grid reference: SN (22) 705 705.

Common and waste: 5000 acres (Act).

Gwnnws Common. Partly in parishes of Lledrod, Llangwyryfon, Llanilar, Rhostïe, Llanddeiniol, Llanychaearn, and Llanrhystud.

Commissioners: John Cheese of Lyonshall; David Joel Jenkins of Lampeter; Hugh Hughes of Aberystwyth. Surveyor: John Hughes of Aberystwyth (all from act).

Award: Not known

Principal allottees: Act names only the King.

Notes: JJ 2315. The award was not completed by 1835, when doubts were raised as to whether one would be valid. (see Davies, 1976, and NLW MSS Crosswood Deeds and Documents II, 1068.)

(ii)   See Llanfihangel-y-Creuddyn (49005).

LLANBADARN ODWYN   See Llangeitho (49013).

LLANBADARN TREFEGLWYS
(i)   See Llanrhystud (49014).

(ii)   See Blaenpennal (49001).

49006   LLANBEDR PONT STEFFAN (LAMPETER)

Order 1854.   Award 1858.
Provisional Order of 10 June 1853, confirmed by 17-18 Vic. c. 9.

Grid reference: SN (22) 574 482.

Common and waste: 53 acres (order), 54 acres (actual).

Manor of Doldremont.

Valuer: John Rees of Pencarreg.

Award: PRO (Kew) MAF 1/368.

Principal allottees: Two exceeded 10 per cent - J. S. and J. B. Harford (38 acres) and the Overseers of the Poor (5½).

Notes: JJ 2354.

LLANDDEINIOL (LLANDINOL)   See Gwnnws (49004).

LLANDDEWIBREFI

49009   (i)   Order 1863.   Award 1888.

Provisional Order of 14 November 1861, confirmed by 26-27 Vic. c. 39.

Grid reference: SN (22) 663 553.

Common and waste: 17,000 acres (order), 16,040 acres (actual).

Mynydd Llanddewi, in the townships (now parishes) of Gorwydd, Prysg and Carfan, Garth and Ystrad, Gogoyan, Doethie Pysgotwr and Doethie Camddwr.

Valuer: John Morgan Davies of Froodvale.

Award: i) PRO (Kew) MAF 1/259 (maps) and 1/1006 (award); ii) NLW Card C C Deposit 7 (maps) and 19 (award).

Principal allottees: Twenty-five received over 100 acres. The major ones were - representatives of J. Inglis Jones (4656 acres), the Ecclesiastical Commissioners (1269 acres), the representatives of Daniel Evans (738 acres), those of Mary Franks (493 acres), and J. W. Willis-Bund (480 acres). Willis-Bund was also joint owner of a further 228 acres.

Papers: CRO holds some legal papers.

Notes: JJ 2373

(ii)   See Blaenpennal (49001).

(iii) See Llangeitho (49013).

49010   LLANFAIR CLYDOGAU

Order 1853. Award 1859.
Provisional Order of 21 April 1853, confirmed by Vic. c. 120.

Grid reference: SN (22) 624 513.

Common and waste: 1631 acres (order), 1610 acres (actual).

Llanfair Mountain.

Valuer: David Davies of Froodvale.
Surveyor: Samuel Evans of Llanrhystud

Award: i) PRO (Kew) MAF 1/237; ii) PRO (Chancery) LRRO 1/60 and MR 614; iii) NLW Card C C Deposit 8; iv) PRO (Chancery) CREST 6/179 A (amendment, to correct errors and omissions in original award).

Principal allottees: Only Baron Carrington (672 acres) exceeded 10 per cent.

Notes: JJ 2353.

LLANFIHANGEL GENAU'R-GLYN
   (i)   See Ysgubor-y-coed (49011).

   (ii)   See Llangynfelyn (49012).

   (iii) See Llangynfelyn (49008).

49005 LLANFIHANGEL-Y-CREUDDYN

Order 1860. Award 1866.
Provisional Order of 15 December 1859, confirmed by 23-24 Vic. c. 17.

Grid reference: SN (22) 750 690.

Common and waste: 6524 acres (award), 6523 acres (actual).

Rhospeiran, Ty-gwyn, Blaenmeherin, Nant Rhys Dyliw, Dolchenog, Nant-y-cae, Bwlch Gwallter. Partly in Gwnnws parish.

Valuer: Richard Wakeford Attree of Westminster.

Award: i) PRO (Kew) MAF 1/58 and MR 810; ii) NLW Card C C Deposit 6; iii) PRO (Chancery) LRRO 1/3081 (plan).

Principal allottees: William Chambers received 6291 acres.

Notes: JJ 2366.

49013 LLANGEITHO

Order 1856. Award 1859.
Provisional Order of 26 June 1856, confirmed by 19-20 Vic. c. 106.

Grid reference: SN (22) 620 598.

Common and waste: 655 acres (order), 641 acres (actual).

Llangeitho Common. Partly in parishes of Llanbadarn Odwyn and Llanddewibrefi.

Valuer: David Davies of Froodvale.
Surveyor: Samuel Evans of Llanrhystyd.

Award: i) PRO (Kew) MAF 1/370; ii) NLW Card C C Deposit 10.

Principal allottees: Only two owners exceeded 5 per cent - the Overseers of the Poor (41 acres) and the unspecified Lord of the Manor (36 acres).

Notes: JJ 2359.

LLANGWYRYFON (LLANGRIOYTHON, LLANGWYRYDDON) See Gwnnws (49004).

LLANGYNFELYN

49012 (i) Act 53 Geo. III c. 71 (not printed) 1813. Award 1847.

Grid reference: SN (22) 658 925.

Common and waste: 10,000 acres (act), 3685 acres (award), 4505 acres (actual).

Cors Fochno. Partly in Llanfihangel Genau'r-glyn.

Commissioners: Two were appointed, but a complex series of changes took place:
a) Thomas Hassall of Cilrhiw died, and was replaced by Charles Hassall of Eastwood, who also died. His replacement, David Joel Jenkins of Lampeter, was removed for failing to act, and replaced by Richard Griffithes of Bishops Castle.
b) Richard Jones of Pantirrion, the second commissioner, resigned and was replaced by Robert Williams of Tŷ-Coch, who in turn was replaced for inaction. His successor was Thomas Jones the Younger, of Penbryn. Finally, in 1845, Thomas Jones Griffithes of Bishops Castle was made sole commissioner.
Surveyor: Charles Mickleburgh of Montgomery.

Award: i) NLW Card C C Deposit 5; ii) CRO ADX 105 (for Genau'r-glyn only).

Principal allottees: Two exceeded 10 per cent - Pryse Pryse (957 acres) and the heirs of Matthew Davies (478 acres).

Notes: JJ 2306 and 2324. Act was amended by 5 Geo.
IV c. 29, 1824. An award of 1829 was blocked by an
action in the Court of Chancery (see Davies,
1976).

49008 (ii) Order 1862. Award 1872.
Provisional Order of 12 December 1861, confirmed by
25-26 Vic. c. 94.

Grid reference: SN (22) 675 895.

Common and waste: 2245 acres (award), 1979 acres
(actual).

Ceulan-y-maes-mawr and Llangynfelyn Common. Partly
in Llanfihangel Genau'r-glyn.

Valuer: Daniel Thomas of Frondeg in Llanbadarn
Fawr.

Award: i) PRO (Kew) MAF 1/232 (map) and 1/1021
(award); ii) NLW Card C C Deposit 3 and 4.

Principal allottees: Matthew Lewis Vaughan Davies
received 1925 acres.

Notes: JJ 2370.

LLANILAR

49007 (i) Order 1858. Award 1861.
Provisional Order of 25 March 1858, confirmed by
21-22 Vic. c. 61.

Grid reference: SN (22) 636 725.

Common and waste: 114 acres (award and actual).

Rhos-y-garth Common in Rhostïe.

Valuer: David Davies of Froodvale.

Award: i) PRO (Kew) MAF 1/814; ii) PRO
(Chancery) MPE 128; iii) NLW Castle Hill MSS
Deeds and Docs 847, 2577.

Principal allottees: Four exceeded 10 per cent -
Sarah Elizabeth Williams (24 acres), James Loxdale
(22 acres), Earl Vaughan (15 acres), and the Queen
(15 acres).

Notes: JJ 2362.

(ii) See Gwnnws (49004).

49014 LLANRHYSTUD (LLANRHYSTYD)

Act 52 Geo. III c. 61 (not printed) 1812. Award 1816.

Grid reference: SN (22) 538 697.

Common and waste: 5000 acres (Act), 4300 acres (BoA).

Manor of Haminiog. Mynydd Bach, Rhos Anhuniog, Rhos Cilcennin, Rhosybiswel Commons. Partly in parishes of Llansanffraid, Llanbadarn Trefeglwys, and Cilcennin.

Commissioners: Charles Hassall of Eastwood, who died and was replaced by John Cheese of Lyonshall; David Joel Jenkins of Lampeter.
Surveyor: John Hughes of Aberystwyth.

Award: NLW Card C C Deposit 20.

Principal allottees: Seven received over 100 acres - Revd Alban Thomas Jones Gwynne (417 acres), John Lloyd (408 acres), Lord Lisburne and Hon. John Vaughan jointly (404 acres), William Lewis (146 acres), the King (145 acres), Elizabeth Hughes (134 acres), and Susanna Saunders (123 acres).

Papers: PRO (Chancery) CREST 6/145.

Notes: JJ 2294.

(ii) See Gwnnws (49004).

(iii)   See Blaenpennal (49001)

LLANSANFFRAID
(i)   See Llanrhystud (49014).

(ii)   See Blaenpennal (49001).

LLANYCHAEARN   See Gwnnws (49004).

LLEDROD   See Gwnnws (49004).

49015 NANCWNLLE

Order 1850. Award 1857.
Provisional Order of 7 February 1850, confirmed by
  13-14 Vic. c. 66.

Grid reference: SN (22) 576 587.

Common and waste: 592 acres (award), 591 acres
  (actual).

Mynydd Bach Twrgwyn and Mynydd Bach Pen uwch.

Valuer: John William Rees of Pencarreg in Llanilar.

Award: i) PRO (Kew) MAF 1/439; ii) NLW Card C C
  Deposit 12.

Principal allottees: Only the Bishop of St Davids
  (70 acres) exceeded 10 per cent.

Papers: PRO (Chancery) CREST 6/179A.

Notes: JJ 2349.

RHOSTÏE
  (i)   See Gwnnws (49004).

  (ii) See Llanilar (49007).

49011 YSGUBOR-Y-COED (SCYBORYCOED)

Order 1862. Award 1872.
Provisional Order of 12 December 1861, confirmed by
  25-26 Vic. c. 94.

Grid reference: SN (22) 630 890.

Common and waste: 240 acres (order), 241 acres
  (actual).

Valuer: Daniel Thomas of Frondeg in Llanbadarn
  Fawr.

Award: i) PRO (Kew) MAF 1/1018; ii) NLW Card C C
  Deposit 13.

Principal allottees: Revd Lewis Charles Davies
  received all but 3 acres.

Notes: JJ 2370.

CARMARTHENSHIRE

ABERGWILI (ABERGWILLY)

50001 (i) Act 54 Geo. III c. 35 (not printed) 1814. Award 1819.

Grid reference: SN (22) 440 209.

Common and waste: 1762 acres or 'thereabouts' (award), 1401 acres (actual).

Lands in Whitigader Manor. Partly in Llanegwad and Llanllawddog parishes.

Commissioner: Robert Smith of Carmarthen.
Surveyor: Richard Bowen Williams of Moreb (correctly 'Horeb') in Pembrey.

Award: CRO AE 13.

Principal allottees: Five exceeded 50 acres – William Misters (238 acres), George Morgan (89 acres), Lord Cawdor (70 acres), the late Jeremiah Price (66 acres), and Richard Bowen Williams (55 acres).

Notes: JJ 2309.

50002 (ii) Order 1851. Award 1855.
Provisional Order of 11 October 1850, confirmed by 14-15 Vic. c. 2.

Grid reference: SN (22) 440 209.

Common and waste: 43 acres (award), 42 acres (actual).

Valuer: William Goode of St Clears.

Award: i) PRO (Kew) MAF 1/704; ii) CRO AE 11.

Principal allottees: Three exceeded 5 acres – the Bishop of St Davids (8 acres), Walter O. Price (7 acres), and the Overseers of the Poor (6 acres).

Notes: JJ 2350.

ABER-NANT

50003 (i) Order 1865. Award 1868.
Provisional Order of 16 December 1864, confirmed by 28-29 Vic. c. 20.

Grid reference: SN (22) 330 232.

Common and waste: 56 acres (order), 51 acres (actual).

Abernant Common in Upper Hamlet.

Valuer: John Lewis of Gwarallt in Llandefeilog.

Award: i) PRO (Kew) MAF 1/929; ii) CRO AE 4.

Principal allottees: Only one exceeded 10 acres, Jacob Jones (11 acres).

Notes: JJ 2377.

50004 (ii) Order 1860. Award 1862.
Provisional Order of 19 January 1860, confirmed by 23-24 Vic. c. 55.

Grid reference: SN (22) 340 231.

Common and waste: 83 acres (award and actual).

Clawdd-coch Common.

Valuer: John Lewis of Gwarallt in Llandefeilog.

Award: i) PRO (Kew) MAF 1/820; ii) CRO AE 23.

Principal allottees: Two exceeded 20 acres - David Davies (34 acres) and the late George Rees Bevan (19 acres).

Notes: JJ 2367.

CAEO (CAYO)   See Llansadwrn (50022).

CEFN ARTHEN   See Llanfair-ar-y-bryn (50006).

50005 CILRHEDYN

Order 1865. Award 1873.
Provisional Order of 24 November 1864, confirmed by 28-29 Vic. c. 39.

Grid reference: SN (22) 278 349.

Common and waste: 2230 acres (award), 2232 acres (actual).

Rhos Llangeler, Rhos Cilrhedin, Rhos Penboyr, Cwmhiraeth, Waun Gilwen. Partly in parishes of Llangeler and Pen-boyr.

Valuer: John Morgan Davies of Froodvale.

Award: i) PRO (Kew) MAF 1/518 (map) and /1084 (award); ii) CRO AE 19.

Principal allottees: Only one exceeded 10 per cent, the Earl of Cawdor (802 acres).

Notes: JJ 2378.

CLAWDD-COCH   See Aber-nant (50004).

GRANGE   See Llangeler (50019).

GWYDDGRUG   See Llanfihangel-ar-arth (50007).

50008 KIDWELLY ST MARY (CYDWELI)

Act 11 Geo. IV c. 16 1830. Award 1854.

Grid reference: SN (22) 409 067.

Common and waste: 2000 acres (Act), 918 acres (actual).

The Grange Common. Partly in parishes of Kidwelly St Ishmael (Cydweli Llanismel) and Pembrey (Pen-bre).

Commissioner: Complex wrangling took place. William Hand of Molleston, the original commissioner, was removed for neglect and incompetence. Rival groups then elected a Mr Parry and a Dr Thomas Evans, and the former began work. After challenges by the latter and his supporters, the Enclosure Commissioners stepped in and appointed David Davies of Froodvale, technically as a valuer.
Surveyor: Edmund Blathwayt.

Award: i) CRO AE 3 and AE 7; ii) NLW Ashburnham 110; iii) PRO (Chancery) LRRO 1/3156 (plan).

Principal allottees: None received 10 per cent. Largest was Edward Crompton Lloyd Fitzwilliams (73 acres).

Papers: PRO (Kew) MAF 25/8/B4003 contains material on dispute, and on later stages of enclosure.

Notes: JJ 2327, JJ2339, JJ2342. Act amended by 8-9 Vic. c. 11, 1845, and finally enclosed under Provisional Order of 21 January 1848, confirmed by 11-12 Vic. c. 27, 1848.

50009 LLANARTHNE (LLANARTHNEY)

Act 51 Geo III c 165 1811. Award 1820.

Grid reference: SN (22) 534 202.

Common and waste: 5080 acres (award), 4041 acres (actual).

Partly in parishes of Llan-non, Llandybïe, and Llanfihangel Aberbythych.

Commissioners: Charles Hassall of Eastwood, Thomas Hassall of Kilrhue, and Richard Jones of Pantirrion were originally appointed. Both Hassalls died, and Jones also ceased to act. The award was completed by John and William Hand, both of Llangunnor.

Award: CRO AE 17 and Dynevor 60A.

Principal allottees: Three exceeded 200 acres – the Earl of Cawdor (883 acres), Lord Dynevor (253 acres), and George Kirtley (209 acres).

Notes: JJ 2283 and 2291. Act amended by 52 Geo. III c. 165, 1812.

LLANBOIDY See St Clears (50028).

LLANDEFEISANT See Llandeilo-fawr (50013).

LLANDEILO-FAWR (LLANDILOFAWR)

50012   i) Act 57 Geo. III c. 63 (not printed) 1817. Award 1818.

Grid reference: SN (22) 629 222.

Common and waste: 500 acres (Act).

Manordilo. Partly in parish of Talley (Talyllychau).

Commissioner: George Morris of Llangennech.
Surveyor: John Bowen of Llandilofawr.

Award: i) CRO AE 24 (award), and AE 15 (plan); ii) PRO (Chancery) LRRO 1/3131 (plan).

Principal allottees: Act records only the King.

Notes: JJ 2319.

50013   (ii) Act 54 Geo. III c. 44 (not printed) 1814. Award 1814.

Grid reference: SN (22) 629 222.

Common and waste: area not stated.

Manor of Llandilo Patria. Partly in parishes of Llangadock, Llanfynydd and Llandefeisant.

Commissioner: Charles Hassall of Tenby was named in the bill, but died before the Act was passed, and was replaced by George Morris of Llangennech.
Surveyor: John Bowen of Llandilofawr.

Award: CRO AE 16.

Principal allottees: Act records Bishop of St Davids, Edward Pryse Lloyd, Thomas Taylor, Rice Williams, William Morgan, Charles Morgan, John Philipps and Revd David Protheroe.

Notes: JJ 2310.

(iii)   See Llansadwrn (50022).

LLANDYBÏE (LLANDEBYE)   See Llanarthne (50009).

50011 LLANDYFAELOG (LLANDEFEILOG)

Order 1858. Award 1860.
Provisional Order of 30 December 1857, confirmed by 21-22 Vic. c. 8.

Grid reference: SN (22) 415 119.

Common and waste: 51 acres (award and actual).

Mynydd Eiddole and Waunllefrith.

Valuer: David Davies of Froodvale.

Award: i) PRO (Kew) MAF 1/809; ii) CRO AE 20.

Principal allottees: Two exceeded 10 per cent – George Talbot (25 acres) and Edward Morris Davies (16 acres).

Notes: JJ 2361.

50010 LLANDDAROG

Act 50 Geo. III c. 37 (not printed) 1810. Award ?

Grid reference: SN (22) 503 166.

Common and waste: 600 acres (Act), 700 acres (BoA).

Mynyddcover, Wayntrellwyd, and Mynyddkerrig. Partly in Llangynnwr (Llangunnor) parish.

Commissioners: Charles Hassall of Eastwood; Thomas Hassall of Kilrhue (appointed in Act).

Award: Not known.

Principal allottees: Act records Lord Cawdor, William O. Brigstock, Lord Dynevor, Sir John Stepney, Sir William Paxton, and Richard M. Philipps. The lord of the manor received one fourteenth.

Notes: JJ 2272.

LLANEDI   See Llanelli (50015).

LLANEGWAD
(i) See Llanfynydd (50020).

(ii) See Abergwili (50001).

LLANELLI (LLANELLY)

50014 (i) Act 47 Geo. III c. 107 1807. Award 1810.

Grid reference: SS (21) 543 987.

Common and waste: 600 acres (Act), 400 acres (BoA).

Berwick Hamlet.

Commissioners: Charles Hassall of Eastwood; William Hopkins of Llangennech.

Award: i) CRO AE 14; ii) PRO (Chancery) LRRO 1/3150 (plan).

Principal allottees: Act records Lord Cawdor and the Borough of Llanelly. The Lord of the Manor received one fourteenth.

Notes: JJ 2251.

50015 (ii) Act 52 Geo. III c. 57 (not printed) 1812. Award 1843.

Grid reference: SN (22) 506 005.

Common and waste: Area not given, but substantial.

Partly in parishes of Llangennech and Llanedi.

Commissioner: Thomas Hassall of Kilrhue, who died and was replaced by John Wedge of Goodig.
Surveyor: Richard Bowen Williams of Horeb in Pembrey.

Award: i) CRO AE 1 B; ii) PRO (Chancery) LRRO 1/3151, 1/3152, and 1/3153 (plans).

Principal allottees: Act records only Lord Cawdor.

Notes: JJ 2293.

50006 LLANFAIR-AR-Y-BRYN

Order 1859. Award 1867.
Provisional Order of 19 January 1859, confirmed by 22 Vic. c. 3.

Grid reference: SN (22) 815 434.

Common and waste: 179 acres (award), 176 acres (actual).

Cefn Arthen, in Rhandirisa hamlet.

Valuer: William Morgan of Llandingal.

Award: i) PRO (Kew) MAF 1/309; ii) CRO AE 12.

Principal allottees: Four exceeded 20 acres – Edward Jones (40 acres), George W. R. Watkin (27 acres), Crawshay Bailey (24 acres), and Mary and Margaret Thomas (13 acres).

Notes: JJ 2363.

LLANFIHANGEL ABERBYTHYCH   See Llanarthne (50009).

LLANFIHANGEL-AR-ARTH (YE-ROTH)

50016 (i) Order 1853. Award 1857.
Provisional Order of 10 November 1852, confirmed by 16-17 Vic. c. 120.

Grid reference: SN (22) 502 355.

Common and waste: 432 acres (award), 442 acres (actual).

Mynydd Llanfihangel and Cwmmins Penyllwyd-coed.

Valuer: John Lewis of Cuncoed in Llandefeilog.

Award: i) PRO (Kew) MAF 1/355; ii) PRO (Chancery) LRRO 1/26 and MR 616; iii) PRO (Chancery) CREST 6/179A (extract); iv) CRO AE 1. v) NLW Room C 17.

Principal allottees: Only one exceeded 10 per cent, Thomas Lloyd and Charles Richard Longcroft (51 acres).

Notes: JJ 2353. Listed in confirming Act as 'y-eroth'.

50007 (ii) Order 1868. Award 1872.
Order confirmed by 31-32 Vic. c. 31.

Grid reference: SN (22) 465 357.

Common and waste: 1118 acres (award and actual).

Grange of Gwyddgrug.

Valuer: Edward David of Radyr Court, Radyr.

Award: i) PRO (Kew) MAF 1/104; ii) PRO (Chancery) LRRO 1/3143; iii) CRO AE 5; iv) NLW Room C 16.

Principal allottees: Four exceeded 10 per cent – John W. M. G. Hughes (170 acres), John Jones (168 acres), the Queen (156 acres), and the Revd Josiah Rees (113 acres).

Notes: JJ 2381.

LLANFIHANGEL CILFARGEN   See Llanfynydd (50020).

50018   **LLANFIHANGEL RHOS-Y-CORN**

Act 51 Geo. III c. 57 (not printed) 1811. Award ?

Grid reference: SN (22) 530 340.

Common and waste: 3000 acres (Act), 900 acres (BoA).

Forest, Clyncothy and Bwlchcynbyd Manors. Partly in Llanybydder parish.

Commissioners: Charles Hassall of Eastwood; George Thomas of Brechfa (from Act).

Award: Not known.

Principal allottees: Act records John Williams Hughes and nineteen others by name. The Lord of the Manor received one fourteenth.

Notes: JJ 2286.

LLANFYNYDD

50020   (i) Act 52 Geo. III c. 62 1812. Award ?

Grid reference: SN (22) 559 276.

Common and waste: 1500 acres (Act).

Cathiniog. Partly in parishes of Llanegwad, Llangathen and Llanfihangel Cilfargen.

Commissioner: Thomas Hassall of Kilrhue, who died and was replaced by Arthur Davies of Oswestry.
Surveyor: John Bowen of Llansadwrn.

Award: Not known

Principal allottees: Act records only the King.

Papers: PRO (Chancery) CREST 6/108. Plan in PRO (Chancery) LRRO 1/3102 of limits of commons enclosed, as sworn by Henry Jones, aged 63, in 1863.

Notes: JJ 2295.

(ii)   See Llandeilo Fawr (50013).

LLANGADOCK (LLANGATWG)   See Llandeilo Fawr (50013).

LLANGATHEN   See Llanfynydd (50020).

LLANGELER

50017 (i) Order 1852. Award 1855.
Provisional Order of 3 September 1851, confirmed by 15-16 Vic. c. 2.

Grid reference: SN (22) 360 390.

Common and waste: 138 acres (award and actual).

Waunmeiros.

Valuer: John Lewis of Kincoed in Llandefeilog.

Award: i)   PRO (Kew) MAF 1/696;   ii)   CRO AE 11A.

Principal allottees: Two exceeded 10 per cent – William Price Lewis (97 acres) and William Strickland (23 acres).

Notes: JJ 2351.

(ii)   See Cilrhedyn (50005).

50019 (iii) Order 1848. Award 1854.
Provisional Order of 21 January 1848, confirmed by 11-12 Vic. c. 27.

Grid reference: SN (22) 374 394.

Common and waste: 494 acres (award and actual).

Grange Common in Grange hamlet.

Valuer: Thomas Saunders of Lampeter.

Award: i) PRO (Kew) MAF 1/676; ii) CRO AE 10.

Principal allottees: Five exceeded 10 per cent – the Revd Thomas Lewis (120 acres), David Davies and Arthur Saunders (57 acres), David Williams (54 acres), Daniel Prytherch (50 acres), and Mrs Nicholls (50 acres).

Notes: JJ 2342. Map dated 1853.

LLANGENNECH See Llanelli (50015).

LLANGYNNWR (LLANGWNNOR, LLANGUNNOR) See Llanddarog (50010).

50021 LLANGYNOG (LLANGUNNOG)

Act 48 Geo. III c. 10 (not printed) 1808. Award 1812.

Grid reference: SN (22) 340 163.

Common and waste: 2300 acres (Act), 1500 acres (BoA).

Partly in Llansteffan parish.

Commissioners: Charles Hassall of Eastwood; Richard Jones of Panthirion; George Morris of Llangennech. Jones did not sign award.

Award: CRO AE 22 and AE 26.

Principal allottees: Act records James Hamlyn Williams, William Morris, Thomas Morris, Ambrose Goddard, George Meares, and William Lloyd. The Lord of the Manor received one fourteenth.

Notes: JJ 2256.

LLANLLAWDDOG   See Abergwili (50001).

LLAN-NON (LLANNON)   See Llanarthne (50009).

50022   **LLANSADWRN**

Act 49 Geo. III c. 16 (not printed) 1809. Award 1817.

Grid reference: SN (22) 695 315.

Common and waste: 1500 acres (Act), 1083 acres (award), 1450 acres (actual).

Mynydd Llansadwrn and Waungynnydd Common. Partly in parishes of Llandeilo Fawr and Caeo.

Commissioners: Charles Hassall of Eastwood, who died, and was replaced by John Bowen of Froodvale, who had been surveyor; William Hopkin of Llangennech.

Award: i) CRO Glassbrook 4/87 (1817) and 3/57 (1816); ii) NLW D T M Jones Colln 5806.

Principal allottees: Two exceeded 10 per cent – Sir Thomas Foley (350 acres) and Lord Robert Seymour (200 acres).

Notes: JJ 2265.

LLANSTEFFAN   See Llangynog (50021).

LLANYBYDDER (LLANYBYTHER)

50023   (i) Order 1885. Award 1892.
Provisional Order of 6 March 1885, confirmed by 48-49 Vic. c. 58.

Grid reference: SN (22) 520 440.

Common and waste: 1890 acres (order), 1812 acres (award and actual).

Valuer: John Francis of Carmarthen.

Award: i) PRO (Kew) MAF 1/17; ii) PRO (Chancery) LRRO 1/3129; iii) CRO AE 9.

Principal allottees: Three exceeded 10 per cent –
Colonel Herbert Davies Jones (460 acres), the
Queen (228 acres), and David Long Price (203
acres).

Notes: JJ 2390.

(ii)   See Llanfihangel Rhos-y-corn (50018).

50024 LLAN-Y-CRWYS (LLAN-CRWYS)

Order 1850. Award 1854.
Provisional Order of 9 March 1850, confirmed by
13-14 Vic. c. 66.

Grid reference: SN (22) 645 454.

Common and waste: 1057 acres (award), 1060 acres
(actual).

Llanycrwys Common.

Valuer: David Davies of Froodvale in Conwil Cayo.

Award: i) PRO (Kew) MAF 1/466;   ii) CRO AE 6;
iii) NLW Rhys Dafydd Williams D C;   iv) PRO
(Chancery) LRRO 1/3134 (plan).

Principal allottees: Two exceeded 10 per cent –
George Lloyd (173 acres) and Sir David Davies (149
acres).

Papers: PRO (Chancery) CREST 6/179A.

Notes: JJ 2349.

LLAWRBANTE   See Tre-lech a'r Betws (50025).

MYNYDD EIDDOLE   See Llandyfaelog (50011).

PEN-BOYR (PEMBOYR)   See Cilrhedyn (50005).

PEN-BRE (PEMBREY)   See Kidwelly St Mary (50008).

50026 PENCARREG

Order 1850. Award 1855.
Provisional Order of 7 February 1850, confirmed by 13-14 Vic. c. 66.

Grid reference: SN (22) 535 450.

Common and waste: 2720 acres (award), 2695 acres (actual).

Pencarreg Mountain.

Valuer: John Edwards of Lampeter.

Award: i) PRO (Kew) MAF 1/4; ii) CRO AE 21.

Principal allottees: Four exceeded 200 acres - Colonel Thomas Wood (284 acres), Major-General Sir James Cockburn (245 acres), Robert Stratton and Mrs Lewis (227 acres), and the Queen (211 acres).

Notes: JJ 2349.

50027 PENDINE (PENTYWYN)

Order 1855. Award 1864.
Provisional Order of 3 January 1855, confirmed by 18-19 Vic. c. 14.

Grid reference: SN (22) 229 088.

Common and waste: 97 acres (award and actual).

Pendine Common.

Valuer: Harry Phelps Goode of Haverfordwest.

Award: i) PRO (Kew) MAF 1/344; ii) CRO AE 8 and AE 25.

Principal allottees: Two exceeded 20 acres - William F. D. Saunders (31 acres) and Sir Thomas Davies Lloyd (23 acres).

Notes: JJ 2355.

RHANDIRISA   See Llanfair-ar-y-bryn (50006).

50028 ST CLEARS (SANCLÊR)

Act 47 Geo. III c. 37 1807. Award ?

Grid reference: SN (22) 281 158.

Common and waste: 283 acres (Act), 216 acres (from plans), 280 acres (BoA).

Manor of St Clears. Partly in Llanboidy parish.

Commissioners: John Howell of Penyrheol; John Waters of Treventy; Charles Hassall of Eastwood (appointed by Act). Map signed by Chas Hassall and Wm Hopkin, 12 May 1809.

Award: None known, but apparently completed c.1809.

Principal allottees: From totals given in plans, four exceeded 10 per cent — the unspecified 'Lord of the Manor' (in fact the King) (30 acres), Lord Milford (27 acres), Hugh Leach (26 acres), and Walter Williams (22 acres).

Papers: Plans in PRO (Chancery) LRRO 1/3135.

Notes: JJ 2252.

TALLEY (TALYLLYCHAU)   See Llandeilo Fawr (50012).

50025 TRE-LECH A'R BETWS

Order 1865. Award 1868.
Provisional Order of 16 December 1864, confirmed by 28-29 Vic. c. 39.

Grid reference: SN (22) 309 266.

Common and waste: 22 acres (award), 21 acres (actual).

Llawrbante Common, otherwise Cwmmins Bach.

Valuer: John Lewis of Kincoed, and later Gwarallt, in Llandyfaelog.

Award: i) PRO (Kew) MAF 1/931; ii) CRO AE 2.

Principal allottees: None received 10 acres. The largest was Lemuel Thomas (7 acres).

Notes: JJ 2377.

DENBIGHSHIRE

ABERGELE

51001   (i)   Act   48 Geo. III c. 83 1808.   Award 1826.

Grid reference: SH (23) 945 776.

Common and waste: 3000 acres (Act), 2278 acres (actual).

Moelfre Mountain, Gallt y felin wynt, Galltwen, Cefn ogo, Abergele Marsh.

Commissioner: John Matthews of Plas yn Llysfaen.
Assistant Commissioner: William Williams of Mold.

Award: i)   PRO (Chancery) LRRO 1/3404;   ii)   CRO QSD/DE/7.

Principal allottees: Five exceeded 100 acres – William Lewis Hughes (723 acres), Lloyd Bamford Hesketh (325 acres), Sir John Williams (149 acres), the King (123 acres), and Elizabeth Gifford (108 acres).

Papers: PRO (Chancery) CREST 6/145.

Notes: JJ 2254.

(ii)   See St Asaph, FLINT (52019).

51002   **BETWS ABERGELE (BETWS-YN-RHOS)**

Act   49 Geo. III c. 129 1809.   Award 1831.

Grid reference: SH (23) 906 735.

Common and waste: 3500 acres (Act).

Commissioners: John Maughan, initially of Hitchin but by award of Barnt Green, Worcestershire; John Matthews of Aberystwyth. Act appointed Josiah Boydell of Ellesmere as Umpire if required.
Assistant Commissioner: William Williams of Mold.

Award: i)   CRO QSD/DE/14;   ii)   PRO (Chancery) LRRO 1/3410 (plan).

Principal allottees: Act records the King, Bishop of St Asaph, Revd Edward Evans, Sir Watkin

Williams Wynn, Sir Edward Pryce Lloyd, John Lloyd Wynne, and Robert W Wynne.

Papers: PRO (Chancery) CREST 6/123.

Notes: JJ 2262.

51003 **BETWS GWERFUL GOCH**

Order 1863. Award 1866.
Provisional Order of 1 January 1863, confirmed by 26-27 Vic. c. 39.

Grid reference: SJ (33) 032 466.

Common and waste: 177 acres (award), 21 acres (actual).

Bettws Hills. CRO lists also as MERIONETHSHIRE, and the parish lies partly in both counties. There is a separate enclosure for Merionethshire (see 54001).

Valuer: Richard Wakeford Attree of Westminster, who replaced John Wilkes Poundley of Kerry, who had resigned.

Award: i) PRO (Kew) MAF 1/912; ii) CRO QSD/DE/28.

Principal allottees: There were only two, Lord William Bagot (21 acres) and an unspecified 'owner of the soil' (3 acres).

Papers: CRO D/GA/974-9.

Notes: JJ 2373.

BRYNEGLWYS   See Llanarmon-yn-Iâl (51009).

CERRIGYDRUDION (CERRIG Y DRUIDION)

51015 (i) Order 1853. Award 1863.
Provisional Order of 5 July 1853, confirmed by 16-17 Vic. c. 120.

Grid reference: SH (23) 954 488.

Common and waste: 4860 acres (order), 4862 acres (actual).

Commons or Crown Wastes.

Valuer: John Wilkes Poundley of Kerry.

Award: i) PRO (Kew) MAF 1/1113; ii) PRO (Chancery) MR 880; iii) CRO QSD/DE/26. iv) PRO (Chancery) LRRO 1/3415 and 1/3416 (plans).

Principal allottees: Two exceeded 10 per cent – Townshend Mainwaring (1040 acres) and Charles Wynne Griffiths Wynne (516 acres).

Notes: JJ 2353.

51019 (ii) Order 1869. Award 1872 and 1877. Provisional Order of 15 June 1865, confirmed by 32-33 Vic. c. 159.

Grid reference: SH (23) 966 446.

Common and waste: 2071 acres (actual).

Tir Abbot Ucha. Possibly partly in Llangwm parish.

Valuer: George Smith of Northampton.

Award: i) PRO (Kew) MAF 1/24; ii) CRO QSD/DE/30.

Principal allottees: There were only three – the Hon. Richard Cavendish (1348 acres), Robert James Sisson (462 acres), and Oliver Evans (261 acres).

Notes: JJ 2383.

(iii) See Llangwm (51017).

CHIRK (Y WAUN) See Llangollen (51016).

CLOCAENOG See Ruthin (51005).

DERWEN See Ruthin (51005).

EFENECHDYD See Ruthin (51005).

51006   EGLWYS-FACH (EGLWYSBACH)

Act   52 Geo. III c. 125 1812. Award 1831.

Grid reference: SH (23) 804 705

Common and waste.

Also in parishes of Llansanffraid Glan Conway and Llaneilian-yn-Rhos. Each parish has a separate award, all with same date. Part of Eglwys-fach lies in CAERNARFONSHIRE.

Commissioners: John Maughan 'late of Luton'; John Matthews of Aberystwyth. Maughan apparently replaced Walter Jones of Cefn Rug. John Calveley of Stapleford was named as Umpire in the Act.
Assistant Commissioner: Josiah Potts of Ollerton, who refused and was replaced by William Williams of Mold.

Award: i)   CRO QSD/DE/12;   ii)   PRO (Chancery) CREST 6/123 (extract);   iii)   PRO (Chancery) LRRO 1/3408 (plan) and 1/3409.

Principal allottees: Act records the King, Bishop of St Asaph, Revd William Parry, and fifteen others.

Notes: JJ 2290.

GYFFYLLIOG   See Ruthin (51005).

51007   HENLLAN

Act   42 Geo. III c. 69 1802. Award 1814.

Grid reference: SJ (33) 022 681.

Common and waste: 8000 acres (Act).

Denbigh Green and Henllan wastes.

Commissioner: John Matthews of Newmarket, later of Plas yn Llysfaen.
Surveyor: Thomas Williams of Henllan.

Award: i)   CRO QSD/DE/3;   ii)   PRO (Chancery) LRRO 1/3405;   iii)   CRO PCD/15/11 (C19 copy).

Principal allottees: Act records the King, Bishop of St Asaph, Revd William Davies Shipley, and seven others.

Papers: i) PRO (Chancery) CREST 6/108; ii) CRO BD/A/94 and /83.

Notes: JJ 2240.

51008 HOLT (LYONS)

Act 57 Geo. III c. 35 1817. Award 1848.

Grid reference: SJ (33) 412 541.

Common and waste: 260 acres (Act). Award does not give details of each lot.

Common Wood.

Commissioner: James Boydell of Rosset, who died and was replaced by George William Chaloner of Holt.

Award: i) PRO (Kew) MAF 1/653; ii) CRO QSD/DE/19; iii) PRO (Chancery) LRRO 1/3398 (plan); iv) CRO DD/DM/442/1.

Principal allottees: Most of land was divided into 64 allotments, to be held in trust and rented to resident burgesses.

Papers: CRO DD/PL/474.

Notes: JJ 2320, 2343, 2348. Act apparently amended by a Provisional Order of 29 January 1846, confirmed by 11-12 Vic. c. 8, 1850.

LLANARMON DYFFRYN CEIRIOG   See Llanymynech (51021).

LLANARMON MYNYDD MAWR   See Llanymynech (51021).

51009 LLANARMON-YN-IÂL

Act 51 Geo. III c. 118 1811. Awards 1815 and 1830.

Grid reference: SJ (33) 190 561.

Common and waste: 'of considerable extent' (Act).

Moel Famau. Partly in parishes of Llandegla and Bryneglwys, and lying partly in FLINT.

Commissioners: Walter Jones of Cefn Rug for Bryneglwys; John Calvely for the rest. Calvely was replaced by Edward Jones Hughes of Plas Onn, originally the surveyor to Jones at Bryneglwys.
Surveyors: Hughes, for Bryneglwys, Edward Rogers of Northop for rest.
Assistant Commissioner: Josiah Potts of Ollerton, who refused and was replaced by William Williams of Mold.

Award: i) CRO QSD/DE/4 (Bryneglwys), QSD/DE/9 (Llandegla), QSD/DE/10 (Llanarmon); ii) CRO QSD/DE/4A (Bryneglws); iii) CROH QS/DE/15 (Llanarmon); iv) CRO PD/43/1/59 (Llanarmon); v) PRO (Chancery) LRRO 1/3370 (plan), 1/3372 and 1/3373.

Principal allottees: Act records Bishop of St Asaph, Sir Thomas Mostyn, Sir Watkin Williams Wynn, the King, and sixteen others.

Papers: i) PRO (Chancery) CREST 6/108; ii) CROH QS/DEM/3 (commissioners' minutes); iii) CRO DD/DM/704/1-2.

Notes: JJ 2278. The award of 1815 covers Bryneglwys, and two in 1830 cover Llandegla and Llanarmon.

LLANDEGLA   See Llanarmon-yn-Iâl (51009).

LLANDUDNO   See Eglwys-Rhos in CAERNARFONSHIRE (48004).

51010   LLANDYRNOG

Act 53 Geo. III c. 149 1813.   Award not known

Grid reference: SJ (33) 108 641.

Common and waste: area not stated (Act).

Partly in parish of Llangwyfan.

Commissioner: John Maughan of Luton (Act).

Award: No record that one was ever made.

Principal allottees: Act records trustee for the Myddeltons, Bishop of Bangor, Revd John Nanney, Richard Butler Clough, and John Madocks.

Notes: JJ 2303.

LLANEILIAN-YN-RHOS   See Eglwys-fach (51006).

51011 LLANELIDAN

Act 49 Geo. III c. 61 1809. Award 1822.

Grid reference: SJ (33) 106 504.

Common and waste: 1200 acres (Act).

Bodlowydd, Bryn Cymme, Llan Trewyn.

Commissioner: Richard Jebb of Chirk. Dodd says 'of Oswestry', but he operated from Chirk by 1822.
Surveyors: Edward Jones Hughes of Mold; John Simon of Ruthin.

Award: CRO QSD/DE/5.

Principal allottees: Act records Bishop of Bangor, Revd Robert Jones, Ruthin Free School, Mary Kenrick, Richard H. Kenrick, and Richard Parry.

Notes: JJ 2261.

LLANFAIR DYFFRYN CLWYD   See Ruthin (51005).

LLANFERRES   See Cilcain in FLINT (52002).

LLANFIHANGEL GLYN MYFYR

51012 (i)   Order 1863. Award 1869.
Provisional Order of 1 January 1863, confirmed by 26-27 Vic. c. 39.

Grid reference: SH (23) 990 493.

Common and waste: 1163 acres (award), 1169 acres (actual).

Llanfihangel Hills. Partly in MERIONETHSHIRE.

Valuer: Abraham Foulkes of Ruabon.

Award: i) PRO (Kew) MAF 1/145 (map) and 1/988 (award); ii) CRO QSD/DE/29; iii) CRO (Merioneth) Z/QR/EN/10 (Z/QR/EN/11 is photocopy); iv) PRO (Chancery) LRRO 1/3430 (plan).

Principal allottees: Two exceeded 10 per cent – Lord Bagot (243 acres) and John Wynne (200 acres).

Papers: CRO D/GA/974-9.

Notes: JJ 2373.

(ii)   See Llangwm (51017).

51013 LLANFWROG

Act   39-40 Geo. III c. 85 1800.   Award 1805.

Grid reference: SJ (33) 114 578.

Common and waste: 900 acres (Act).

Gallteg fa, Coed Marcham, Cefn Collon, Hengoed Common.

Commissioners: Robert Harvey of Dunstal; Josiah Boydell of Rosset and later Cilhendre; Thomas Lovett of Chirk, who was replaced by Thomas Lloyd of Denbigh.

Award: CRO QSD/DE/2.

Principal allottees: Act records trustees of the Myddeltons, Reverend William Parry, Lord Bagot, Sir Watkin Williams Wynn, and Reverend Thomas Youde.

Notes: JJ 2235.

LLANGADWALADR   See Llanymynech (51021).

51014 LLANGERNYW (LLANGERNIEW)

Act   3-4 Vic. c. 11 1840.   Award 1843.

Grid reference: SH (23) 875 675.

Common and waste: 1500 acres (Act).

Commissioner: Francis Marston of Hopesay.

Award: i) CRO QSD/DE/16;   ii)   PRO (Chancery) LRRO 1/3412.

Principal allottees: Act records Bishop of St Asaph, Samuel Sandbach, and Robert William Wynne.

Notes: JJ 2334.

51016 LLANGOLLEN

Act 2-3 Vic. c. 2 1839. Awards 1848 (2), 1849, 1851.

Grid reference: SJ (33) 217 420.

Common and waste, and intermixed lands.

Chirk Honour. Partly in Llansanffraid Glynceiriog parish.

Commissioner: Charles Mickleburgh of Montgomery.
Surveyor: Richard Yates of Whittington.

Award: i) CRO QSD/DE/17 , QSD/DE/22 and QSD/DE/23; ii) CRO PCD/64/31-3;   iii)   CRO D/DM/162/44,46 (maps only);   iv)   NLW Maps C 35.

Principal allottees: Act records Charlotte Myddelton Biddulph, Hon. Frederick West, Sir Watkin Williams Wynne, Robert Myddelton Biddulph, William Ormsby Gore, and Richard Jones.

Notes: JJ 2333. Awards of 6/1/1848, of 1849 and of 1851 refer to Llangollen. That of 19/12/1848 refers to Llansanffraid.

LLANGWM

51017 (i) Order 1863. Award 1869.
Provisional Order of 1 January 1863, confirmed by 26-27 Vic. c. 39.

Grid reference: SH (23) 966 446.

Common and waste: 2999 acres (actual).

Llangwm Hills. Also partly in Cerrigydrudion and possibly Llanfihangel Glyn Myfyr parishes.

Valuer: Richard Wakeford Attree of Ruabon, who died and was replaced by Abraham Foulkes of Ruabon.

Award: i) PRO (Kew) MAF 1/61 (map) and 1/1080
(award);   ii) CRO QSD/DE/27 (maps only).

Principal allottees: Two exceeded 10 per cent –
John Wynne (835 acres), and an unspecified 'Owner
of the Soil' (308 acres).

Papers: CRO D/GA/974-9.

Notes: JJ 2373.

(ii)   See Cerrigydrudion (51019).

LLANGWYFAN   See Llandyrnog (51010).

51020 LLANRWST

Act 52 Geo. III c. 68 (not printed) 1812. Award 1830.

Grid reference: SH (23) 798 616.

Common and waste: 5000 acres (Act).

Lands in Hiraethog. Partly in Gwedir township in CAERNARFONSHIRE.

Commissioners: Walter Jones of Cefn Rug, who died and was replaced by John Matthews of Plasynllysfaen, who in turn died and was replaced by John Maughan of Barnt Green; John Calvely of Stapleford, who died and was replaced by John Matthews of Pen-y-bont and later Aberystwyth.
Assistant Commissioner: Josiah Potts of Ollerton, who refused and was replaced by William Williams of Mold.

Award: i) CRO QSD/DE/8;   ii) PRO (Chancery) LRRO 1/3286 (plan) and 1/3406;   iii) CRO (Caernarfonshire) INC AW 5 (for Gwedir);   iv) CRO PD/1/226 (Gwedir).

Principal allottees: Act records the King, Charles W. Griffith Wynne, Sir Thomas Mostyn, William Edwards, William Roberts, John Wynne Griffiths, Revd Robert Meyrick Humphreys, and Revd J. Ellis.

Papers: PRO (Chancery) CREST 6/123 and 6/145.

Notes: JJ 2297.

51018 **LLANRHAEADR-YNG-NGHINMEIRCH** (listed as **YN KINMERCH**)

Act 54 Geo. III c. 61 (not printed) 1814. Award 1836.

Grid reference: SJ (33) 081 635.

Common and waste: 4966 acres (actual).

Mynydd Llech, Bryn Mulan, Bryn Brion, Moel Gasyth, Nantci, Cefn Main, Foel, Cwmcast, Llech Fared.

Commissioner: Walter Jones of Cefn Rug, who died in 1814 and was replaced Edward Jones Hughes of Plas Onn, who in turn was replaced by Robert Peters of Mold.
Surveyor: John Simon.
Assistant Commissioner: Robert Harvey of Dunstal, who was replaced by John Jones of Plas Issa in Llangar.

Award: i) CRO QSD/DE/15; ii) PRO (Chancery) LRRO 1/3411 (plan).

Principal allottees: Fourteen exceeded 100 acres, of whom five received more than 5 per cent of the total. These five were: Richard Wilding (613 acres), Lord Dinorben (349 acres), the King (332 acres), Lord Bagot (307 acres), and Revd John Jones (295 acres).

Papers: i) PRO (Chancery) CREST 6/145 and /179C; ii) CRO DD/DM/392/2 (commissioners' minutes).

Notes: JJ 2312.

LLANRHAEADR-YM-MOCHNANT   See Llanymynech (51021).

LLANSANFFRAID GLAN CONWY   See Eglwys-fach (51006).

LLANSANFFRAID GLYNCEIRIOG   See Llangollen (51016).

51021 **LLANYMYNECH**

Act 7 Wm IV c. 2 1837. Award 1844.

Grid reference: SJ (33) 150 300.

Open field, common and waste: 22770 acres (actual). Apparently includes some 10 acres of open field.

Townships of Trebrys, Banhadla Ucha, Llangadwaladr, Gartheryn, Llanrhaeadr, Llanarmon, Llanymynech, Henfache, Trellan and Rhiwlas. Partly in parishes of Llanrhaeadr-ym-Mochnant, Llanarmon Mynydd Mawr, Llanarmon Dyffryn Ceiriog, and Llangadwaladr. At the time of enclosure, part lay in SHROPSHIRE.

Commissioners: Richard Yates of Whittington; William Bright of Admaston, who died and was replaced by Charles Mickleburgh of Montgomery.

Award: i)   CRO QSD/DE/18;   ii)   CRO PD/72/1/88-9.

Principal allottees: Forty received over 100 acres, including the Overseers of the Poor of Ruabon (244 acres). The four with over 1000 acres were – Sir Watkin Williams Wynn (4791 acres), the Hon. Frederick West (4459 acres), John Bonnor (1346 acres), and Mrs Frances Roberts (1034 acres).

Notes: JJ 2331.

51023 LLANYNYS

Act 42 Geo. III c. 113 1802. Award 1820.

Grid reference: SJ (33) 102 626.

Common and waste: 600 acres (Act).

Ysceibion.

Commissioners: Charles Barnes Robinson of Hill Ridware; Robert Jones of Ruthin. Both replaced, by Robert Harvey of Dunstal and John Roberts of Ruthin.

Award: i)   CRO QSD/DE/6;   ii)   PRO (Chancery) LRRO 1/3403.

Principal allottees: Act records the King, Lord Bagot, Revd Thomas Roberts, Sir Watkin Williams Wynn, Revd Thomas Youde, and Robert Lloyd.

Papers: PRO (Chancery) CREST 6/145.

Notes: JJ 2241.

51022 LLYSFAEN

Order 1863. Award 1871.
Provisional Order of 12 December 1861, confirmed by 26-27 Vic. c. 18

Grid reference: SH (23) 893 775.

Common and waste: 285 acres (order) 280 acres (actual).

Marian Llysfaen.

Valuer: Thomas Jones of Denbigh, who died and was replaced by Richard Roberts of St Asaph.

Award: i) PRO (Kew) MAF 1/456; ii) CRO (Caernarfon) INC AW 10; iii) PRO (Chancery) LRRO 1/3280 (plan).

Principal allottees: Three exceeded 10 per cent – Anna Williams Wynn (68 acres), the Queen (61 acres), and John Lloyd Wynne (36 acres).

Notes: JJ 2372. Parish was formerly in CAERNARFONSHIRE.

NANNERCH   See Ysgeifiog, FLINT (52018).

51024 NANTGLYN

Order 1852. Award 1854.
Provisional Order of 28 August 1851, confirmed by 15-16 Vic. c. 2.

Grid reference: SJ (33) 005 621.

Common and waste: 2983 acres (award), 2981 acres (actual).

Nantglyn Common.

Valuer: Richard Wakeford Attree of Liss (in fact of Ruabon by this date)

Award: i) PRO (Kew) MR 882; ii) CRO QSD/DE/24. iii) PRO (Chancery) CREST 6/179 pp 71-3, and MR 1768 (extracts only).

Principal allottees: Four exceeded 10 per cent –
Revd Thomas Wynne Edwards (643 acres), John Lloyd
Maurice (421 acres), William Owen (381 acres), and
John Lloyd Wynne (327 acres).

Papers: CRO DD/PN/70.

Notes: JJ 2351.

51005 RUTHIN (RHUTHUN)

Order 1852. Award 1861.
Provisional Order of 8 January 1852, confirmed by
15-16 Vic c 2.

Grid reference: SJ (33) 124 584.

Common and waste: 5600 acres (order), 5606 acres
(actual).

Ruthin Manor. Partly in parishes of Llanfair
Dyffryn Clwyd, Llanelidan, Derwen, Efenechdyd,
Clocaenog, Gyffylliog.

Valuer: Richard Yates of Oswestry, who died and was
replaced by Richard Wakeford Attree of Ruabon.
Surveyors: Samuel Cartwright and John Hughes.

Award: i) PRO (Kew) MAF 1/243 (map) and 1/1014
(award); ii) CRO QSD/DE/25; iii) CRO
PD/37/1/113 (Gyffylliog).

Principal allottees: Three exceeded 300 acres –
Lord Bagot (1272 acres), Frederick Richard West
(529 acres), and Sir Watkin Williams Wynn (310
acres).

Papers: CRO award contains minutes and other
papers.

Notes: JJ 2351.

51004 WREXHAM (WRECSAM)

Act 48 Geo. III c. 16 1808. Award ?

Grid reference: SJ (33) 269 520.

Common and waste: 480 acres (Act), 525 acres
(actual).

Minera.

Commissioner: Josiah Boydell of Rosset.
Surveyor: Richard Jebb of Oswestry.

Award: not known. CRO has extract from award dated 1816 in DD/HB/356. PRO (Chancery) LRRO 1/3371 contains map plus tabulated key (no date).

Principal allottees: Two exceeded 10 per cent – James Topping (109 acres) and Hugh Meredith (79 acres).

Notes: JJ 2260. Act amended by 49 Geo III c 187 1809.

FLINT

BRONINGTON   See Hanmer (52006).

52001   CAERWYS

Act 49 Geo. III c. 130 1809. Award 1850.

Grid reference: SJ (33) 126 728

Common and waste: 1200 acres (Act).

Brickhill Common.

Commissioner: Edward Rogers of Northop, who presumably replaced John Calveley of Stapleford (named in Act).

Award: CRO QS/DE/25 and P/13/1/46.

Principal allottees: Act records the King, Earl of Plymouth, Revd J. Lloyd, Sir Thomas Mostyn, and Samuel Mostyn.

Notes: JJ 2263.

52002   CILCAIN

Act 33 Geo. III c. 92 1793. Award 1801.

Grid reference: SJ (33) 176 652.

Common and waste: 4200 acres (Act). Partly in Llanferres parish, in DENBIGHSHIRE. Act specifies 2400 acres in FLINT, 1800 acres in DENBIGHSHIRE.

Commissioners: Richard Hill of Farley, who resigned and was replaced by Josiah Boydell of Rossett; Josiah Potts of Ollerton; John Matthews of Newmarket.

Award: i) CRO QS/DE/8 and P/14/1/48; ii) CROR QSD/DE/1 and PD/57/1/99; iii) CRO P/14/1/48, and /36; iv) CROR PD/57/1/99; v) PRO (Chancery) LRRO 1/3368 (plan).

Principal allottees: Act records the King, Revd Edward Parry, Revd John Delap, Revd John Lloyd, Richard Hughes Lloyd, John Griffith Williams, Charles Potts, and Catherine Jones Garnons.

Papers: PRO (Chancery) CREST 6/108; CRO QS/DEM/1-2 (commissioners' minutes).

Notes: JJ 2227. Listed by Bowen as Kilken.

COLESHILL FAWR (CWNSYLLT)   See Flint (52005).

CWM (Y CWM)
  (i)   See Newmarket (52014).

  (ii) See Rhuddlan (52017).

52003 DEE ESTUARY (AFON DYFYRDWY)

Act 26 Geo. II c. 35 (Public) 1753. Award ?

Grid reference: SJ (33) 225 765.

Common and waste: 3100 acres (Act).

White Sands.

Commissioner: None recorded.

Award: Probably none made.

Principal allottees: Not given.

Notes: There were several acts, all Public and all concerned with navigation as well as enclosure. Two earlier ones (6 Geo. II c. 30, 1733 and 14 Geo. II c. 8, 1740) seem to have been at least mainly for navigation purposes, and 31 Geo. III c. 88, 1791 (listed by JJ as 2224 and 1329), was effectively an amendment. The Act of 1753 confirmed an agreement between a navigation company, the Lord of the Manor, and commoners.

DISERTH (DYSERTH)
  (i)   See Rhuddlan (52017).

  (ii) See St Asaph (52019).

52004 ELLESMERE

Act 35 Geo. III c. 15 1795. Award 1796.

Grid reference: SJ (33) 413 400.

Common and waste: 90 acres (Act).

Penley township. Penley is now a separate parish, and Ellesmere now lies wholly in SHROPSHIRE.

Commissioner: Thomas Boydell of Trevallyn, who resigned and was replaced by Arthur Davies of Oswestry.

Award: CRO QS/DE/6.

Principal allottees: Act records Phillips Lloyd Fletcher, Lord Kenyon, Sir Thomas Hanmer, and John Kynaston.

Notes: JJ 2231.

52005 FLINT (Y FFLINT)

Act 53 Geo. III c. 69 1813. Award 1830.

Grid reference: SJ (33) 244 730.

Common and waste: 276 acres (Act).

Partly in parish of Coleshill Fawr.

Commissioner: John Calveley of Bruern Stapleford, who died and was replaced by Edward Jones Hughes of Plas Onn.

Award: i) CRO QS/DE/23; ii) PRO (Chancery) LRRO 1/3467 (plan) and 1/3468 (extract)

Principal allottees: Act records the King, Sir Piers Mostyn, Sir Edward Pryce Lloyd, William Lewis Salusbury Trelawny, Bagot Read, and Bryan Cooke.

Papers: CRO D/BJ/371 (commissioner's minutes and accounts).

Notes: JJ 2300.

52006 HANMER

Act 15 Geo. III c. 16 1775. Award 1777 and 1779.

Grid reference: SJ (33) 455 398.

Common and waste: 2000 acres (Act), 3000 acres (Evans).

Fens Heath, Stemmy Heath, Bronington Green, Little Green, Rhos Poeth Green, Horse Moss Green, Talwrn Green, The Arrowry, Braden Heath, Bermoss Green, Bettisfield Moss.

Commissioners: Thomas Boydell of Trevallyn; Thomas Vernon of Oswestry; Thomas Whilton of Tyrley.

Award: i) CRO QS/DE/1 and 2; ii) NLW Cholmeley and Co deposit.

Principal allottees: Act records Sir Walden Hanmer, Phillips Lloyd Fletcher, John Puleston, Sir Richard Parry Price, Lloyd Kenyon, Edward Dymock, Phillip Henry Keay, and Revd John Ravenscroft. Evans (1983-4) records about half went to Hanmer.

Notes: JJ 2214.

HAWARDEN (PENARLÂG)

52007 (i) Act 18 Geo. III c. 90 1778. Award 1781.

Grid reference: SJ (33) 345 655.

Common and waste: 2000 acres (Act).

Saltney Marsh.

Commissioners: Samuel Wyatt of Burton-on-Trent; Edward Stelfox of Sunderland in Bowden; John Earl of Overton.

Award: i) CRO QS/DE/3 and 4; ii) PRO (Chancery) LRRO 1/3513 (plan).

Principal allottees: Act records Revd Sir Stephen Glynne, the Earl of Plymouth, and Ann Whitley. Evans (1983-4) states Glynne received 1005 acres.

Papers: CRO D/BJ/368-70 (Act and commissioners' accounts) and D/DM/69/2 (receipts).

Notes: JJ 2216. JJ also lists 44 Geo. III c. 31 for this enclosure, under 2242. In fact this was really a drainage Act, rather than an amendment in the strict sense of the word.

52008 (ii) Act 38 Geo. III c. 25 1798. Award 1802.

Grid reference: SJ (33) 320 632.

Common and waste: 600 acres (Act).

Warren Mountain in Broughton, Pentrobin, and Pannell (Bannel) townships.

Commissioners: Josiah Boydell of Rossett, later of Cilhendre, Josiah Potts of Ollerton, Thomas Wedge of Sealand.
Surveyor: James Boydell of Llay.

Award: CRO QS/DE/10.

Principal allottees: Act records Sir Stephen Richard Glynne, Earl Grosvenor, Lord Kenyon, Dame Mary Glynne, and Sir George William Prescott.

Papers: CRO D/LA/1-9 (commissioners' minutes and other papers).

Notes: JJ 2234.

52009 HOPE (YR HOB)

Act 31 Geo. III c. 69 1791. Award 1797.

Grid reference: SJ (33) 309 585.

Common and waste: 3500 acres (Act). Turner says 6000 acres, Evans 4053.

Dodleston Moor, Talwrn Green. Partly in parishes of Dodleston and Lower Kinnerton (CHESHIRE) and Higher Kinnerton.

Commissioners: Samuel Weston of Halewood; Richard Hill of Farley, who died but was apparently not replaced; John Thomas of Trevallyn, who died and was replaced by Josiah Boydell of Rossett; Matthew Fletcher of Clifton.
Surveyors: James Heys of Knowsley; Richard Smith of Cheadle.

Award: i) CRO QS/DE/7; ii) CRO (CHESHIRE) Q/DE/2/7; iii) CRO DC/272 (award and plan, Dodleston) and DC/195 (award and plans, Hope).

Principal allottees: Act records Earl of Derby, Earl Grosvenor, Lord Kenyon, Lord Dacre, Grace Trevor, George Boscawen, Sir Stephen Richard Glynne, Sir Richard Brooke, and Sir Edward Lloyd. Derby received 1040 acres (Evans).

Papers: NLW Leeswood Hall MSS; CRO D/LA/11 (commissioners' minutes).

Notes: JJ 2225. A full account of the enclosure is given by Evans (1983-4).

KINNERTON, HIGHER   See Hope (52009).

LLANASA

52010 (i) Act 51 Geo. III c. 149 1811. Award 1846.

Grid reference: SJ (33) 106 816.

Common and waste: 1600 acres (Act).

Gwespyr and Picton Marshes, Axton, Kelston, Gronant, Trelogan Common.

Commissioners: Thomas Wedge of Sealand; John Calveley of Stapleford, who died and was replaced by Edward Rogers of Northop.
Assistant Commissioner: Josiah Potts of Ollerton, who was replaced by William Williams of Mold. Williams in turn died, and was replaced by Edward Williams of Garreglloyd near Mold.

Award: i) CRO QS/DE/24; ii) PRO (Chancery) LRRO 1/3492 (plan) and MR 1768 (outline plan).

Principal allottees: Act records Sir Piers Mostyn, the King, Bishop of St Asaph, Revd Henry Parry, and eight others.

Papers: i) PRO (Chancery) CREST 6/179A; ii) CRO D/GY/88.

Notes: JJ 2280.

52011 (ii) Order 1850. Award 1854.
Provisional Order of 28 June 1849, confirmed by 13-14 Vic c 66.

Grid reference: SJ (33) 120 822.

Common and waste: 159 acres (order), 158 acres (actual).

Picton Marsh.

Valuer: Thomas Jones of Denbigh.

Award: i) PRO (Kew) MAF 1/861; ii) CRO QS/DE/26; iii) CRO D/LA/47; iv) CRO D/DM/100/4 (plan).

Principal allottees: The trustees of Sir Pyers Mostyn received 81 per cent (129 acres).

Notes: JJ 2349.

52012 MELIDEN (ALLT MELYD)

Order 1863. Award 1870.
Provisional Order of 13 March 1862, confirmed by 26-27 Vic. c. 18.

Grid reference: SJ (33) 062 809.

Common and waste: 440 acres (order), 442 acres (actual).

Meliden Hill, Towyn Hill, Prestatyn Hill.

Valuer: George Bell of Rhyl.

Award: i) PRO (Kew) MAF 1/324 (map) and /1102 (award); ii) CRO QS/DE/27.

Principal allottees: Three exceeded 10 per cent - John Dawson (266 acres), Thomas Griffies Dixon (49 acres), and trustees of the Mostyn estate (45 acres).

Notes: JJ 2372.

(ii) See St Asaph (52019).

52013 MOLD (YR WYDDGRUG)

Act 32 Geo. III c. 54 1792. Award 1800.

Grid reference: SJ (33) 237 642.

Common and waste: 4000 acres (Act), 3811 acres (actual). Area may be slightly understated due to defective copy of award.

Commissioners: Samuel Wyatt of Burton-on-Trent, who died and was replaced by Josiah Boydell of Rossett; Josiah Potts of Ollerton; James Calverley of Huntingdon; John Matthews of Newmarket.

Award: CRO QS/DE/9 (part missing).

Principal allottees: Eight exceeded 100 acres – John Giffard (723 acres), Thomas S. Champneys (469 acres), John Lloyd (258 acres), William Wynne (222 acres), Revd Hope Wynne Eyton (212 acres), Trevor Lloyd (194 acres), Gwyllym Lloyd Wardle (190 acres), and Mary Puleston (182 acres).

Papers: CRO D/KK/272-3 (commissioners' minutes).

Notes: JJ 2226 and 2230. Act amended by 34 Geo. III c. 14 1794.

52014 NEWMARKET (TRELAWNYD)

Act 51 Geo. III c. 117 1811. Award 1828.

Grid reference: SJ (33) 091 798.

Common and waste: 80 acres (Act).

Partly in Cwm parish.

Commissioner: John Calveley of Stapleford, who died and was replaced by John Matthews of Pen-y-bont, and later of Clydfane. Matthews had originally been a surveyor.
Surveyors: Matthews, and Edward Jones of Whitford.
Assistant Commissioner: Josiah Potts of Ollerton, who refused and was replaced by William Williams of Mold.

Award: CRO QS/DE/20.

Principal allottees: Act records the King, Sir Thomas Mostyn, Sir Edward Pryce Lloyd, Sir John

Williams, Revd William Davies Shipley, and Barbara Yonge.

Papers: CRO QS/DEM/4 (commissioners' minutes) and D/GW/480-5 (various papers).

Notes: JJ 2277.

52015 NORTHOP (LLANEURGAIN)

Act 7 Geo. IV c. 17 1826. Award 1831.

Grid reference: SJ (33) 245 685.

Common and waste: 120 acres (Act).

Lands in Soughton (Sychdyn) village.

Commissioner: William Williams of Mold.

Award: i) CRO QS/DE/21; ii) CRO P/45/1/339; iii) PRO (Chancery) LRRO 1/3472 (plan).

Principal allottees: Act records the King, William J. Bankes, Revd John C. Conway, Phoebe Lloyd, Susanna Lloyd, Revd Richard Howard, and Phillip Davies Cooke.

Papers: CRO D/GW/480-5 (accounts and minutes) and D/SH/918 and /982-6 (other papers).

Notes: JJ 2325.

52016 OVERTON (OWRTYN)

Order 1869. Award 1874.
Provisional Order of 28 May 1868, confirmed by 32-33 Vic. c. 159.

Grid reference: SJ (33) 373 418.

Common and waste: 34 acres (order and actual).

Lightwood Green and Knolton Bryn.

Valuer: George Farmer of Montgomery.

Award: i) PRO (Kew) MAF 1/1098; ii) CROH NT/M/105 (photocopy).

Principal allottees: One exceeded 10 per cent - Edmund Peel (21 acres).

Notes: JJ 2383. NLW lists this as part of 51019 (Llangwm, DENBIGHSHIRE), but it appears to be a separate enclosure, merely confirmed by the same Act. The date 1877 given in some lists is the date of countersigning in London.

PENLEY (LLANERCH BANNA)   See Ellesmere (52004).

RHUDDLAN

52017 (i) Act 47 Geo. III c. 62 1807. Award 1815.

Grid reference: SJ (33) 005 785.

Common and waste: 1200 acres (Act).

Part of Morfa Rhuddlan. Partly in parishes of St Asaph, Diserth, and Cwm.

Commissioner: John Matthews of Plas-yn-Llysfaen.

Award: i) CRO QS/DE/14;   ii)   CRO P/54/2/26-7.

Principal allottees: Act records the King, Catherine Stapleton, Watkin Williams, Revd William Davies Shipley, Barbara Yonge, and nine others.

Notes: JJ 2250.

(ii)   See St Asaph (52019).

52019 ST ASAPH (LLANELWY)

Act 34 Geo. III c. 110 (Public) 1794. Award ?

Grid reference: SJ (33) 039 744.

Common and waste: 500 acres (Act). Dodd specifies 300 acres in DENBIGHSHIRE.

Part of Morfa Rhuddlan and Towyn Abergele. Partly in parishes of Rhuddlan, Diserth, Meliden, and Abergele (DENBIGHSHIRE).

Commissioners: Acts refer only to trustees, but PRO records indicate work done by Thomas Wedge of Sealand and John Matthews of Newmarket.

Award: Possibly never made, though there is a plan in PRO (Chancery) LRRO 1/3505 dated 1809 and one in CROH QS/DE/19 dated 13 June 1796.

Principal allottees: Act records the King, Catherine Stapleton, Watkin Williams, Revd William Davies Shipley, Barbara Yonge, Bishop of St Asaph, Revd Edward Hughes, Sir Edward Lloyd, and Richard Wilding.

Notes: JJ 2229 and 2301. Amended by Act of 53 Geo. III c. 121 1813.

52020 (ii) Act 48 Geo. III c. 131 1808. Award 1827.

Grid reference: SH (23) 990 770.

Common and waste: 1000 acres (Act).

That part not in the franchise of Rhuddlan. Partly in DENBIGHSHIRE.

Commissioner: John Calveley of Stapleford. Dodd records as followed by Humphreys, but final award drawn up by Timotheus Burd of Cardiston.

Award: CROH QS/DE/18.

Principal allottees: Act records the King, Catherine Stapleton, Watkins Williams, Revd William Davies Shipley, Barbara Yonge, Bishop of St Asaph, and twelve others.

Notes: JJ 2255. Dodd records some allotments made 1810, but no formal award appears for that date.

(iii) See Rhuddlan (52017).

SYCHDYN See Northop (52015).

52021 **TREMEIRCHION (DYMEIRCHION)**

Act 50 Geo. III c. 139 1810. Award 1831.

Grid reference: SJ (33) 082 737.

Common and waste: 1000 acres (award), 571 acres (actual).

Commissioner: John Maughan of Hitchin, and later of Barnt Green.
Surveyor: William Williams (no address given)

Award: i) CRO QS/DE/22; ii) CRO P/65/2/1; iii) PRO (Chancery) LRRO 1/3507 (plan).

Principal allottees: Three exceeded 50 acres – Sir John S. P. Salisbury (130 acres), heirs of Revd Whitehall W. Davies (95 acres), and the King (56 acres).

Notes: JJ 2269.

52022 WHITFORD (CHWITFFORDD)

Act 39-40 Geo. III c. 120 1799. Award 1807.

Grid reference: SJ (33) 146 782.

Common and waste: 2000 acres (Act).

Mynydd Tegeingl.

Commissioner: John Matthews of Newmarket, and later of Plas-yn-Llysfaen.
Surveyor: John Calveley.

Award: i) CRO QS/DE/13; ii) CRO D/GR/1908 (maps).

Principal allottees: Act records Sir Thomas Mostyn, the King, Lord Grey de Wilton, Revd John Gooch, Revd John Foulkes, Sir Edward Pryce Lloyd, David Pennant, Thomas Thomas, Thomas Mostyn Edwards, and Edward Jones.

Notes: JJ 2237.

52018 YSCEIFIOG

Act 39-40 Geo. III c. 116 1800. Award 1805 .

Grid reference: SJ (33) 153 715.

Common and waste: 3500 acres (Act).

Partly in Nannerch parish in DENBIGHSHIRE.

Commissioner: John Matthews of Newmarket, and later of Plas-yn-Llysfaen.
Assistant Commissioner: Josiah Potts of Ollerton
Surveyor: Robert Piercy of Mold.

Award: i) CRO QS/DE/12; ii) CRO P/43/1/3; iii) CRO P/43/1/1 (award only); iv) CRO D/GR/1907 (maps).

Principal allottees: Act records Watkin Williams, the King, Earl Grosvenor, and nine others.

Papers: PRO (Chancery) CREST 6/108.

Notes: JJ 2236. Wrongly listed by Bowen as 'Ysllifrog and Nannerd'.

GLAMORGAN

53001 ABERDARE (ABERDÂR)

Order 1857. Award 1869.
Provisional Order of 4 June 1857, confirmed by 20-21 Vic. c. 30.

Grid reference: SN (22) 945 035.

Common and waste: 3370 acres (order), 3351 acres (actual).

Hirwaun Common. Partly in Ystradyfodwg parish.

Valuer: Edward David of Radyr Court.

Award: i) PRO (Kew) MAF 1/5 (map) and /1007 (award); ii) CRO Q/DP/254 and /337.

Principal allottees: Only one exceeded 10 per cent, the trustees of the Marquess of Bute (784 acres).

Notes: JJ 2360.

53002 CARDIFF (CAERDYDD)

Act 41 Geo. III c. 113 1801. Award 1809.

Grid reference: SO (32) 175 798.

Common and waste: 1200 acres (Act), 1039 acres (award).

Great and Little Heaths (alias Mwynydd Buchan) and Wain Dyval. In parishes of St John the Baptist, Cardiff, Llandaff, Whitchurch, and Roath.

Commissioners: Thomas Browne of Luton; Henry Hollier of Cardiff; Thomas Morgan of Cardiff.
Surveyor: Thomas Browne the Younger of Luton.

Award: CRO Q/DP/248.

Principal allottees: Act records Marquis of Bute, Earl of Windsor, and Borough of Cardiff.

Notes: JJ 2360. There was also a long wrangle over Leckwith, Canton and Ely Commons (PRO, Kew, MAF 25/99/LO/N560) which culminated in the enclosure of about 0.3 acre in 1935.

COED-PEN-MAEN   See Eglwysilan (53005).

COETY HIGHER

53013   (i)   Order 1882.   Award 1883.

Grid reference: SN (22) 930 840.

Common and waste: area not stated, but small.

Coity Wallia.

Valuer: None.

Award: i)   PRO (Kew) MAF 2/17 and /19;   ii)   CRO Q/DP/474 and /475.

Notes: JJ not given. Part of the common was taken for a bridge and other works, under the Railway Compensation Commissioner's Orders. Possibly admissable as an enclosure.

53003   (ii)   Order 1920.   Award 1936.
Confirmed by 9-10 Geo. V c. 70.

Grid reference: SN (22) 930 840.

Common and waste: area not stated.

Coity Wallia. Partly in parishes of Pencoed, Coychurch Higher, and St Bride's Minor.

Valuer: W. B. Horne.

Award: i)   PRO (Kew) MAF 1/200;   ii)   CRO Q/DP/916.

Notes: JJ not given. Possibly really to be classified as a regulation, though PRO classification indicates an enclosure.

53004   **COLWINSTON (TREGOLWYN)**

Order 1868.   Award 1871.
Provisional Order of 15 February 1866, confirmed by 31-32 Vic. c. 31.

Grid reference: SS (21) 940 755.

Common and waste: 65 acres (order), 70 acres (actual).

Golden Mile Common.

Valuer: William Williams of St Bride's Minor.

Award: i)   PRO (Kew) MAF 1/658;   ii)   CRO Q/DP/338.

Principal allottees: Two exceeded 10 per cent - Hubert de Burgh Thomas (20 acres) and Thomas Bowen (18 acres).

Notes: JJ 2381.

COYCHURCH HIGHER (LLANGRALLO)   See Coety Higher (53003).

53005 EGLWYSILAN

Order 1857. Award 1861.
Provisional Order of 4 June 1857, confirmed by 20-21 Vic. c. 30.

Grid reference: ST (31) 125 925.

Common and waste: 136 acres (order and actual).

Coed-pen-maen.

Valuer: Evan Williams David of Radyr.

Award: i)   PRO (Kew) MAF 1/568;   ii)   CRO Q/DP/201.

Principal allottees: Four exceeded 10 per cent - Richard Bassett (49 acres), the Earl of Bute (29 acres), William Watkin Bassett (19 acres), and Baron Dynevor (18 acres).

Notes: JJ 2360.

GOSTON (TRE-OS)   See Llan-gan (53006).

HIRWAUN   See Aberdare (53001).

53007 LOUGHOR (CASLLWCHWR)

Act 3-4 Wm IV c. 25 1833. Award 1835.

Grid reference: SS (21) 566 981.

Common and waste: 600 acres (Act).

Commissioner: William Bevan of Swansea.

Award: CRO Q/DP/249 and Q/DP/250.

Principal allottees: Act records Duke of Beaufort, and Borough of Loughor.

Notes: JJ 2330.

LLANBLETHIAN (LLANFLEIDDAN) See Pendoylan (53011).

LLANDAFF (LLANDAF) See Cardiff (53002).

53006 LLAN-GAN (LLANGAN)

Order 1855. Awards 1860 and 1862.
Provisional Order of 25 January 1855, confirmed by 18-19 Vic. c. 14.

Grid reference: SS (21) 957 777.

Common and waste: 215 acres (order and actual).

Manors of Penlline, Goston and Langan.

Valuer: James Peachey Williams of Bristol.

Award: i) PRO (Kew) MAF 1/68; ii) CRO Q/DP/220 B and 251.

Principal allottees: Only one exceeded 10 per cent, John Richard Homphray (111 acres).

Notes: JJ 2355, which he records as CARMARTHENSHIRE.

53008 LLANGYFELACH

Order 1882. Award 1897.

Grid reference: SN (22) 655 075.

Common and waste: area not stated.

Mynydd-y-Gwair Common. Under the Commons Compensation Act, and apparently also the Swansea Corporation (Water) Act, 1884.

Valuer: None.

Award: i) CRO Q/DP/637; ii) MAF 2/21.

Principal allottees: Common rights eliminated, and commoners given money compensation.

Notes: JJ not given, but listed as an enclosure by CRO. Parts of Llangyfelach Common were also enclosed, 1000 square yards for a tramway (1930) and 4.75 acres for a road (1938). See PRO (Kew) MAF 25/99/LG7937.

LLANHARRY (LLANHARI)   See Pendoylan (53011).

LLANISHEN (LLANISIEN)   See Cardiff (53002).

LLANSANNOR (LLANSANWYR)   See Pendoylan (53011).

NEW FOREST (near COWBRIDGE)   An enclosure by agreement, sometimes listed as parliamentary since an act was needed to settle a dispute over manorial boundaries.

53009 NEWTON NOTTAGE (DRENEWYDD YN NOTAIS)

Order 1860. Award 1864.
Provisional Order of 17 May 1860, confirmed by 23-24 Vic. c. 55.

Grid reference: SS (21) 840 790.

Common and waste: 855 acres (order), 856 acres (actual).

Backs Common, Cleviston Common and Newton Down, in manors of Pembroke, Loughor and Herbert.

Valuer: James Peachey Williams of Bristol.

Award: i) PRO (Kew) MAF 1/289 (map) and /974 (award); ii) CRO Q/DP/212, /213, /247, /252.

Principal allottees: Four exceeded 10 per cent - Sir Ivor Birke Guest (254 acres), Revd Edward Doddridge Knight (175 acres), Revd Charles Rumsey Knight (129 acres), and the late Sir Josiah John Guest (103 acres).

Notes: JJ not given.

PEN-COED   See Coety Higher (53003).

53011   PENDOYLAN (PENDEULWYN)

Order 1856.   Award 1863.
Provisional Order of 17 January 1856, confirmed by 19-20 Vic. c. 11.

Grid reference: ST (31) 060 767.

Common and waste: 800 acres (order), 753 acres (actual).

Mynydd-y-Glew and Ystradowen Commons in Talyvan manor. Partly in parishes of Welsh St Donats, Ystradowen, Llanblethian, Llansannor, and Llanharry.

Valuer: James Peachey Williams of Bristol.

Award: i)   PRO (Kew) MAF 1/162 (map) and /1116 (award);   ii)   CRO Q/DP/211.

Principal allottees: Three exceeded 10 per cent - Spencer and Elizabeth Sophia Ricketts (189 acres), Rowland Fothergill (142 acres), and the representatives of the late Sir Joseph Bailey (76 acres).

Notes: JJ 2358.

PENLLINE (PEN-LLIN)   See Llan-gan (53006).

ROATH (Y RHATH)   See Cardiff (53002).

ST BRIDE'S MINOR (LLANSANFFRAID-AR-OGWR)   See Coety Higher (53003).

ST LYTHAN'S (LLWYNELIDDON)   See Wenvoe (53012).

53010   SWANSEA (ABERTAWE)

Act 2 Geo. III c. 7 1762.   Award NONE.

Grid reference: SS (21) 656 929.

Common and waste: 750 acres (Act), 600 acres (BoA).

Town Hill and Burroughs.

Commissioner: None.

Award: None. Act contains terms of award.

Papers: Papers relating to the enclosure in U.C.W., Swansea, and Beaufort Collection, NLW. Act lists as 'Town Hall'.

Notes: JJ 2213.

53012 WENVOE (GWENFÔ)

Order 1857. Awards 1861 and 1863.
Provisional Order of 1 May 1856, confirmed by 20-21 Vic. c. 30.

Grid reference: ST (31) 110 737.

Common and waste: 180 acres (order), 178 acres (actual).

St Lythan's Down.

Valuer: Evan Williams David of Radyr.

Award: i) PRO (Kew) MAF 1/904; ii) CRO Q/DP/220 and Q/DP/229 (amendment).

Principal allottees: Two exceeded 10 per cent - the representatives of the late Robert Francis Jenner (109 acres) and John Bruce Pryce (36 acres).

Notes: JJ 2360.

WELSH ST DONATS (LLANDDUNWYD) See Pendoylan (53011).

WHITCHURCH (YR EGLWYS NEWYDD) See Cardiff (53002).

YSTRADOWEN See Pendoylan (53011).

YSTRADYFODWG (YSTRAD RHONDDA) See Aberdare (53001).

MERIONETHSHIRE

54001 BETWS GWERFUL GOCH (BETWS GWERFIL GOCH)

Order 1865. Award 1869.
Provisional Order of 11 May 1865, confirmed by 28-29 Vic. c. 39.

Grid reference: SJ (33) 033 466.

Common and waste: 878 acres (order and actual).

Betws Commons. The parish also lies partly in DENBIGHSHIRE, for which there was a separate enclosure (51003).

Valuer: Abraham Foulkes of Ruabon.

Award: i) PRO (Kew) MAF 1/491 (map) and /937 (award); ii) CRO Z/QR/EN/8 (/9 is a copy).

Principal allottees: Three exceeded 10 per cent - Lord Bagot (161 acres), John Wynne (135 acres), and Revd David Roberts (106 acres).

Notes: JJ 2378.

54002 DOLGELLAU (DOLGELLEY)

Act 51 Geo. III c. 162 1811. Award 1821.

Grid reference: SH (23) 728 179.

Common and waste: 600 acres (Act).

Partly in Llangelynnin parish.

Commissioner: Josiah Boydell of Cilhendre.
Assistant Commissioner: Walter Jones of Cefn Rug.

Award: CRO Z/QR/EN/17 (Z/QR/EN/15, Z/QR/EN/16, Z/QR/EN/18 copies and extracts).

Principal allottees: Act records the King, Griffith Howel Vaughan, John Kennedy, Sir Robert Williams Vaughan, Richard Richards, and Edward Edwards.

Papers: PRO (Chancery) CREST 6/123.

Notes: JJ 2282.

54003 GWYDDELWERN

Act 50 Geo. III c. 52 (not printed) 1810. Award 1825.

Grid reference: SJ (33) 074 467.

Common and waste: 13,497 acres (award), 13,498 acres (actual).

In hamlets of Gwyddelwern, Rug, and Glyndyfrdwy. Partly in parish of Llansanffraid Glyndyfrdwy.

Commissioners: Josiah Boydell of Cilhendre. Richard Jebb of Chirk was also named in the original Act, for Gwyddelwern only, but apparently resigned, leaving Boydell to complete on his own.
Surveyor: Thomas Roberts of Wern Lodge.

Award: i)   CRO Z/QR/EN/7;   ii)   NLW Salusbury Deposit.

Principal allottees: Nineteen owners exceeded 100 acres, of which three exceeded 500. These were Griffith Howell Vaughan (6472 acres), the representatives of R. H. Lloyd (1141 acres), and Edward Lloyd (517 acres). The allotment for the poor of Llanraiadr was 344 acres.

Notes: JJ 2273.

54004 LLANABER

Act 50 Geo. III c. 56 (not printed) 1810. Award 1836.

Grid reference: SH (23) 599 180.

Common and waste: 17374 acres (Lewis).

Rhuddalt Common, Barmouth Marsh, Morfa Mawr, Gottell-y-Wern, Garth, Mynydd Llanbedr, Rhos y caeran, Ystyllen, Coed Ystumgwern, Llanddwywe Common, Gwyllt Common, Llanaber Common, Cwmysgyba, Pen-y-rhiw goch. Partly in parishes of Llanddwywe, Llanenddwyn, Llanbedr, Llanfair.

Commissioner: Walter Jones of Cefn Rug, who died and was replaced by Josiah Boydell of Rossett. Jones was also Assistant Commissioner.
Surveyor: Robert Williams of Llandegai.

Award: i) CRO Z/QR/EN/4 (/3 and /5 are copies); ii) PRO (Chancery) LRRO 1/3549 and MPE 118 (plans).

Principal allottees: Act records the King, Mary Jane Ormsby, Robert Williams Vaughan, and Revd Francis Perry.

Papers: PRO (Chancery) CREST 6/123.

Notes: JJ 2274.

LLANBEDR   See Llanaber (54004).

54005   LLANDANWG

Act 46 Geo. III c. 21 1806.   Award 1827.

Grid reference: SH (23) 569 282.

Common and waste: 1600 acres (Act).

Morfa Harlech, Mochras Sands, Morfa Felin, Cefn Goch Common. Partly in parish of Llanfihangel y Traethau.

Commissioners: Walter Jones of Cefn Rug, who died and was replaced by William Williams of Dolgelley; James Royle of Caermelwr, who died in 1826 and was probably not replaced.
Surveyor: Robert Williams of Llandegai.

Award: i)   CRO Z/QR/EN/6 (part only, 1840: photocopy);   ii) PRO (Chancery) LRRO 1/3597 (copy plan) and 1/3598, and MR 802 pt 1.

Principal allottees: Act records the King, Sir Thomas Mostyn, Mary Jane Ormsby, and Revd John Nanney.

Notes: JJ 2244. Apparently additional drainage award, 1840.

LLANDDWYWE   See Llanaber (54004).

LLANELLTUD   See Llanfachreth (54006).

LLANENDDWYN   See Llanaber (54004).

54006 LLANFACHRETH

Act 49 Geo. III c. 66 (not printed) 1809. Award 1817.

Grid reference: SH (23) 755 225.

Common and waste: 14,060 acres (Lewis).

Nannau-uwch-yr-afon, Nannau-is-yr-afon, and Llanelltud manors. Partly in Llanelltud parish.

Commissioner: Robert Williams of Llandegai.

Award: CRO Z/QR/EN/17 (Z/QR/EN/18-/20 copies and extracts).

Principal allottees: Act records the King, Sir Robert Williams Vaughan, Griffith Howel Vaughan, William Oakeley, and William Lloyd.

Papers: PRO (Chancery) CREST 6/145.

Notes: JJ 2267.

LLANFAIR   See Llanaber (54004).

LLANFIHANGEL GLYN MYFYR   See DENBIGHSHIRE (51012).

LLANFIHANGEL-Y-TRAETHAU
(i)   See Llandanwg (54005).

(ii)   See CAERNARFONSHIRE (48012)

LLANFROTHEN   See CAERNARFONSHIRE (48012).

LLANGELYNNIN   See Dolgellau (54002).

LLANSANFFRAID GLYNDYFRDWY   See Gwyddelwern (54003).

RUG (Y RUG)   See Gwyddelwern (54003).

TYWYN (TOWYN)

54007 (i)   Act 45 Geo. III c. 68 1805.   Award 1809.

Grid reference: SH (23) 574 015.

Common and waste: 912 acres (Act), 672 acres (actual).

Morfa Towyn, in the township of Faenol.

Commissioner: Thomas Chapman of Richmond, who resigned and was replaced by Griffith Griffiths of Dolgellau. Bowen records Charles Hassall of Narberth as Chapman's replacement. Presumably he in turn resigned.
Surveyor: John Davies of Pennal

Award: i) NLW Towyn U.D.C. Deposit; ii) CRO Z/QR/EN/12 (photocopy) and Z/QR/EN/13 (abstracts and map).

Principal allottees: Two exceeded 10 per cent – Edward Corbet (395 acres) and Edward Scott (98 acres).

Notes: JJ 2243.

54008 (ii) Act 46 Geo. III c. 51 1806. Award 1818.

Grid reference: SH (23) 611 038.

Common and waste: 123 acres (Act).

Gwyddelfynydd.

Commissioner: Charles Hassall of Eastwood, who died and was replaced by Richard Griffithes of Bishop's Castle.
Surveyor: John Davies of Pennal.

Award: CRO Z/QR/EN/14 (abstract).

Principal allottees: Act Records the King, Sir Robert Williams Vaughan, Edward Corbet, and William Wynne.

Papers: PRO (Chancery) CREST 6/108.

Notes: JJ 2247.

TRAETH MAWR   See CAERNARFONSHIRE (48012).

MONMOUTHSHIRE

BISHTON (TREFESGOB)
  (i)   See Magor (55007).

  (ii)   See Undy (55011).

CALDICOT

55001 (i) Order 1858. Award 1859.
Provisional Order of 17 December 1857, confirmed by 21–22 Vic. c. 8.

Grid reference: ST (31) 484 886.

Open fields: 244 acres (actual).

Valuer: James Peachey Williams of Bristol.

Award: i) PRO (Kew) MAF 1/159; ii) CRO Q/INC AW 14.

Principal allottees: None received as much as 25 acres, or 10 per cent of total. Largest single allottee was William Bennett (22 acres).

Notes: JJ 2361.

  (ii)   See Shirenewton (55009).

CWMCARVAN (CWMCARFAN)   See Wentwood (55012).

55002 **CWMYOY (CWM-IOU)**

Act 53 Geo. III c. 41 (not printed) 1813. Award ?

Grid reference: SO (32) 299 233.

Common and waste: 4000 acres (Act).

'Two parcels of waste'.

Commissioners: David Davies of Llangattock (Crickhowell) and Henry Price of Hereford.
Surveyor: Samuel Joseph Harris of Hereford.

Award: Whereabouts unknown.

Principal allottees: Not known. Act records only Walter Savage Landor.

Papers: CRO D.591.32.A.26.

Notes: JJ 2305.

55003 IFTON (IFFTWN)

Act 16 Geo. III c. 77 1776. Award ?

Grid reference: ST (31) 466 880.

Common and waste, and possibly also some open field and meadow: 780 acres, of which about 220 were Ifton Moors (Act).

Commissioners: Francis Burton of Aynho, John Watts of Sulgrave, and Robert Weston of Brackley.

Award: Whereabouts unknown.

Principal allottees: Not known. Act records Jane Rooke, Revd Llewelyn Llewelyn, Sir Charles Kemeys Tynte, and Edward Rumsey Bradbury.

Notes: JJ 2215.

LLANDEVENNY See Magor (55007).

LLANDOGO See Wentwood (55012).

55004 LLANGYBI (LLANGIBBY)

Act 48 Geo. III c. 66 (not printed) 1808. Award 1809.

Grid reference: ST (31) 340 985.

Common and waste and common meadow: 399 acres (actual).

Common Coed y Pane, Forest, and a common meadow, in Tregrug manor.

Commissioner: Thomas Fulljames of Hasfield Court. Surveyor: Robert Wright Hall of Cirencester.

Award: CRO Q/INC AW 1.

Principal allottees: Six exceeded 30 acres - John Lewis junior (72 acres), William Morgan (65 acres), Revd J.A. Williams (45 acres); Capel Leigh (44 acres), William Adams Williams (30 acres), and William Nichol (30 acres).

Papers: NLW (minutes).

Notes: JJ 2258. The Act was officially 'not printed', but an unofficial printed copy exists in CRO.

LLANISHEN (LLANISIEN)   See Wentwood (55012).

LLANVIHANGEL NEAR ROGGIETT

55005 (i)   Order 1851.   Award 1855.
Provisional Order of 20 June 1850, confirmed by 14-15 Vic. c. 2.

Grid reference: ST (31) 451 878.

Common and waste: 83 acres (order), 88 acres (award), 82 acres (actual).

Rogiet and Minutes Common.

Valuer: Thomas Davis of Warminster.

Award: i)   PRO (Kew) MAF 1/418;   ii)   CRO Q/INC AW 10.

Principal allottees: Sir Charles Morgan Robinson Morgan (73 acres).

Notes: JJ 2350.

(ii)   See Shirenewton (55009).

MAGOR (MAGWYR)

55006 (i)   Order 1853.   Award 1854.
Provisional Order of 2 July 1852, confirmed by 16-17 Vic. c. 3.

Grid reference: ST (31) 425 870.

Open fields, common and waste: 155 acres (award), 151 acres (actual).

Upper, Middle and Lower Fields, Magor.

Valuer: James Peachey Williams of St Werburgh in Bristol.

Award: i)   PRO (Kew) MAF 1/1052;   ii) CRO Q/INC AW 9.

Principal allottees: Two exceeded 10 per cent – William Perry Herick (49 acres) and William Phillips (29 acres).

Notes: JJ 2352.

55007 (ii) Order 1853. Award 1856.
Provisional Order of 11 October 1850, confirmed by 15-16 Vic. c. 2.

Grid reference: ST (31) 428 858.

Common and waste: 760 acres (order), 744 acres (actual).

Wastes of the manors of Magor and Redwick, Duram and Ragland, Magor and Green Moor, Salisbury and Magor le Green Moor, and Redwick. Partly in parishes of Redwick, Wilcrick, Magor, Undy, Bishton, and Llandevenny.

Valuer: James Peachey Williams of Bristol.

Award: i)   PRO (Kew) MAF 1/160;   ii) PRO (Chancery) MR 623;   iii) CRO Q/INC AW 11, 12, 13.

Principal allottees: Only one exceeded 10 per cent, William Phillips (85 acres).

Notes: JJ 2351.

MITCHEL TROY (LLANFIHANGEL TRODDI)   See Wentwood (55012).

NEWPORT (CASNEWYDD-AR-WYSG)   Listed by JJ (1667 and 2357). 18-19 Vic. c. 41 (L and P) enabled corporation to buy out interest of Freemen in Newport Marshes. Not regarded here as a genuine enclosure.

PENALT (PEN-ALLT)   See Wentwood (55012).

REDWICK

55008 (i) Order 1850. Award 1852.
Provisional Order of 7 January 1850.

Grid reference: ST (31) 412 841.

Common and waste, possibly including some meadow: 325 acres (award), 326 acres (actual).

Broadmead, Readymead, Cocks Furlong and Barelands.

Valuer: James Peachey Williams of Bristol.

Award: i) PRO (Kew) MAF 1/93; ii) CRO Q/INC AW 3 and 4.

Principal allottees: Three received over 10 per cent – Daniel Baker (93 acres), William T. Jones and Henry T. Jones (38 acres), and William Phillips (37 acres).

Notes: Not listed by JJ. Award states that prior confirmation by Parliament not required, as lands qualify under General Act of 1845. A Provisional Order should not have been needed in this case.

(ii) See Magor (55007).

ROGGIETT
(i) See Shirenewton (55009).

(ii) See Llanvihangel Rogiet (55005).

55009 SHIRENEWTON (DRENEWYDD GELLI-FARCH)

Order 1850. Award 1853.
Provisional Order of 18 December 1849, confirmed by 13-14 Vic. c. 8.

Grid reference: ST (31) 479 935.

Common and waste: 1300 acres (order), 1302 acres (actual).

Caldicot Moor, Rogiet Moor, Ben Acre, Common Sea, Earlswood Common, Mynydd Bach, and Cwm Wood. Partly in parishes of Undy, Llanvihangel Roggiett, Roggiett, and Caldicot.

Valuer: James Peachey Williams of Bristol.

Award: i)   PRO (Kew) MAF 1/116;   ii)   CRO Q/INC AW 5, 6 and 7;   iii) PRO (Chancery) DL 45/4 (part), MR 439.

Principal allottees: Three received over 10 per cent – Sir Charles Morgan Robinson Morgan (240 acres), William Bevan (170 acres), and Robert Sharp (155 acres). The Duchy of Lancaster and the Duke of Beaufort received negligble amounts.

Notes: JJ 2348.

TINTERN (TYNDYRN)   See Wentwood (55012).

TRELECH (TRYLEG)   See Wentwood (55012).

UNDY (GWNDY)

55010 (i)   Order 1853.   Award 1854.
Provisional Order of 2 July 1852, confirmed by 16-17 Vic. c. 3.

Grid reference: ST (31) 430 870.

Common fields: 130 acres (award), 129 acres (actual).

Valuer: James Peachey Williams of Bristol.

Award: i)   PRO (Kew) MAF 1/642;   ii)   CRO Q/INC AW 8.

Principal allottees: Three received over 10 per cent – Sir Charles Morgan Morgan (32 acres), John N. Hawkins (24 acres), and David Carruthers (15 acres).

Notes: JJ 2352.

55011 (ii)   Order 1853.   Award ?
Provisional Order of 13 July 1853, confirmed by 16-17 Vic. c. 120.

Grid reference: ST (31) 430 870.

Common and waste: 232 acres (order).

Partly in Bishton parish.

Valuer: ?

Award: Not known.

Principal allottees: Not known.

Notes: JJ 2353.

(iii) See Shirenewton (55009).

(iv) See Magor (55007).

55012 WENTWOOD

Act 50 Geo. III c. 212 1810. Award 1821.

Grid reference: SO (32) 500 055.

Common and waste: 4200 acres (Act), 5285 acres (actual, plus 959 acres of old enclosures and encroachments redistributed).

Manor of Trelleck. Land in parishes of Cwmcarvan, Llandogo, Llanishen, Mitchel Troy, Trelech, Penalt, Tintern.

Commissioner: Thomas Fulljames of Hasfield Court.
Surveyor: David Davies of Llangattock (Crickhowell).

Award: CRO Q/INC AW 2.

Principal allottees: Two exceeded 10 per cent of the open land - Duke of Beaufort (2103 acres), and Thomas and William Adams Williams (585 acres). Beaufort also received 182 acres for encroachments, but had voluntarily relinquished 167 acres of detached lands. He subsequently sold parts of his allotments.

Notes: JJ 2271. An extremely complex enclosure, involving multiple exchanges of land, and many sales and resales. 306 parties were involved, the largest number known to the author in either England or Wales.

55013 WHITSON

Order 1867. Award 1870.
Provisional Order of 28 March 1867, confirmed by 30-31 Vic. c. 71.

Grid reference: ST (31) 381 835.

Common and waste: 44 acres (order and actual).

Whitson Common.

Valuer: James Peachey Williams of Bristol.

Award: i)   PRO (Kew) MAF 1/617.   ii)   CRO Q/INC AW 15.

Principal allottees: Two exceeded 10 per cent - William Phillips (24 acres) and George Gray Rous (5½ acres).

Notes: JJ 2380.

WILCRICK (CHWILGRUG)   See Magor (55007).

MONTGOMERYSHIRE

56001 ABERHAFESB

Act 36 Geo. III c. 17 1796. Awards 1803, 1805, 1806, 1807, 1815, 1818.

Grid reference: SO (32) 158 933.

Common and waste: 15,000 acres (Act).

Manors of Cedewain, Hopton and Overgorther. Partly in the parishes of Betws, Llandysul, Llanllwchaearn, Llanmerewig, Llanwyddelan, Manafon, Newtown, Berriew, Churchstoke, and Kerry.

Commissioners: Thomas Matthews of Shelderton; Thomas Colley of Cefngwifed; Thomas Jones of Lymore. Matthews and Colley both resigned before 1815, and were replaced by Valentine Vickers (junior) of Cranmere and John Dyer of Cefngwifed. Surveyor: Richard George of Montgomery, who was replaced by John Humphreys of Tyn-y-coed; John Evans; William Pugh (addresses not given).

Award: i) NLW Mont C C 1, 4, 5, 18, 25, 29, 30, 31F, 32, 33, 35, 36-40. 34 is a copy of 4, and 47 of 33; ii) NLW Powis Castle M91, M95-M107.

Principal allottees: Act records Earl of Powis, Revd John Pryce, and eleven others.

Notes: JJ 2232.

ALBERBURY See Bausley (56002). Alberbury lies in SHROPSHIRE, but part of the ecclesiastical parish lay in Wales.

56002 BAUSLEY

Act 2-3 Wm IV c. 7 1831. Award 1835.

Grid reference: SJ (33) 323 148.

Common and waste: 237 acres (Act).

Bausley Hill. Dodd records as in Alberbury parish, of which Bausley was formerly a township.

Commissioner: William Wyley of Admaston.

Award: NLW Mont C C 41.

Principal allottees: Act records Francis Knyvett Leighton, All Souls Oxford, and Revd Richard Webster Huntley.

Notes: JJ 2328.

BERRIEW (ABERRIW, BERRIW)   See Aberhafesb (56001).

BETWS   See Aberhafesb (56001).

BRYN POSTIG   See Llangurig (56013).

BUTTINGTON (TAL-Y-BONT)   See Churchstoke (56004).

CAEREINION, CASTLE (CASTELL CAEREINION)
 (i) See Llanfair Caereinion (56011).

 (ii) See Llanlugan (56016).

CARNO   See Llanidloes (56015).

CHURCHSTOKE (YR YSTÔG)

56004 (i) Act 20 Geo. III c. 31 1780.   Award ?

Grid reference: SO (32) 234 911.

Common and waste: 70 acres (Act).

Gwern-y-mynydd, in manors of Teirtref and Hopton. In townships of Aston, Castlewright, Mellington, and Upper Hopton, partly in parishes of Mainstone and Lydham (SHROPSHIRE).

Commissioners: Richard Price of Knighton; Thomas Matthews of Shelderton; Thomas Hale of Copthorn (from Act).

Award: Not known. Possibly never completed.

Principal allottees: Act records Earl of Powis, John Oakeley, Revd Herbert Oakeley, Revd Samuel D'Elbeuf Edwards, Edmund Plowden, Hospital of Clun, Eleanor Lewis, Thomas Browne, Thomas Morris, John Thomas, and Revd Phillip Morris.

Notes: JJ 2217. Dodd says in parishes of Buttington and Welshpool, but Act makes no reference to either.

56003 (ii) Order 1848. Award 1853.
Provisional Order of 2 November 1846, confirmed by 11-12 Vic. c. 27.

Grid reference: SO (32) 271 940.

Common and waste: 750 acres (order), 761 acres (actual).

Partly in Hurdley parish.

Valuer: Charles Mickleburgh of Montgomery.

Award: i) PRO (Kew) MAF 1/538; ii) NLW Mont C C 11.

Principal allottees: Three exceeded 10 per cent – John Owen (212 acres), the Earl of Powis (98 acres) and William Urwick (87 acres).

Notes: JJ 2342.

(iii) See Aberhafesb (56001).

56006 FORDEN (FFORDUN)

Act 1-2 Geo. IV c. 49 (not printed) 1821. Award 1825.

Grid reference: SJ (33) 228 011.

Common and waste: 240 acres (Act).

Long Mountain, Forden Heath, Fron, and Lower Gro, in Tempsîter manor (alias Teirtref). Lands lay in Kilkewydd township.

Commissioner: Thomas Jones junior of Penbryn (Act).
Surveyor: Charles Mickleburgh of Montgomery.

Award: Present whereabouts unknown (Act specified one copy to church and one to Archdeacon of Salop).

Principal allottees: Act records Revd Joseph Corbett, Panton Corbett, Richard Pryce, Richard Edmunds, Richard Atcherley, Shadrach Edwards, Thomas Vaughan, William Rowson, Nathaniel Price, and others.

Notes: JJ 2323.

GLYNBROCHAN   See Llangurig (56014).

GLYNGYNWIDD (GLYNGYNWYDD)   See Llangurig (56014).

GUILSFIELD (CEGIDFA)

56005 (i) Act 28 Geo. III c. 49 1788. Awards 1799 and 1800.

Grid reference: SJ (33) 219 117.

Open field (610 acres), meadow (140 acres), and common and waste (3709 acres) (all actual). The award also involved substantial reallocation of land already enclosed, and overall redistributed 4846 acres. Dodd gives 3000 acres, while the Act says 2600 acres.

Strata Marcellina (Strata Marcella, or Ystrad Marchell), Tir-y-mynech, and Deuddwr. Partly in parishes of Pool (Welshpool), Meifod, Llandrinio, Llandysilio, and New Chapel.

Commissioners: Thomas Matthews of Shelderton; John Bishton of Kilsall; Henry Bowman of Knockin.
Surveyor: T. B. Plescins of Pool, and later of Crackley Bank. Samuel Botham of Uttoxeter, Arthur Davies of Oswestry and Thomas Kyffin of Copthorn appear also to have been involved.

Award: i)   NLW ENC 12, 21, 24. 19 is a duplicate of 12; ii)   NLW Powis Castle M90.

Principal allottees: Eight exceeded 100 acres, two of whom exceeded 200. The two were Sir William Poulteney (558 acres) and the Earl of Powis (239 acres).

Papers: Copy of Act in CRO M/DX/14/120.

Notes: JJ 2221. Act gives names as Streetmarshal, Tirymynech, and Deytheur.

(ii)   See Welshpool (56019).

HURDLEY   See Churchstoke (56003).

56007 HYSSINGTON

Order 1848. Award 1855.
Provisional Order of 8 January 1847, confirmed by 11-12 Vic. c. 27.

Grid reference: SO (32) 312 941.

Common and waste: 450 acres (order), 464 acres (actual).

Hyssington Marsh, Pwlley Green, Cefn Common, Llan Bank, Maypole Bank, and Hyssington Bank in Hyssington township, and Mucklewick Hill, Little Common, Goniting, and Bridge Green in Mucklewick township. Hyssington parish then lay partly in SHROPSHIRE.

Valuer: Thomas Jones Griffithes of Bishop's Castle.

Award: i) PRO (Kew) MAF 1/359; ii) NLW Mont C C 3. iii) NLW Powis Castle M122.

Principal allottees: Two exceeded 10 per cent - Richard Medlicott (131 acres) and Robert Bridgman More (87 acres).

Notes: JJ 2342.

KERRY (CERI)
  (i)   See Aberhafesb (56001).

  (ii) See Mochdre (56017).

KINNERLEY Now SHROPSHIRE. The enclosure fell within the English part.

LLANDINAM See Llanidloes (56015).

LLANDRINIO See Guilsfield (56005).

LLANDYSILIO See Guilsfield (56005).

LLANDYSUL See Aberhafesb (56001).

56008 LLANERFYL

Act 55 Geo. III c. 100 (not printed) 1815. Awards 1826 and 1829.

Grid reference: SJ (33) 032 098.

Common and waste: 11,575 acres (Act). The 1826 (Llanerfyl) award covers 4624 acres (actual).

Coedtalog, Cenewill (Cnewyll), Crane (Craen), Cefnllys, Llangadfan, Blowty, Cyffin, Moel Feliarth, Bryngwaeddau (Bryngwaeddan). Partly in Llangadfan parish. Bowen lists as Caereinion Uwchcoed, the name of the manor.

Commissioner: Valentine Vickers junior of Cranmere.
Surveyor: Thomas Kyffin of Copthorn.

Award: i)   NLW Mont C C 13;   ii)   NLW Rm C 24; iii) NLW Powis Castle M120, M121.

Principal allottees: Act lists Viscount Clive, Sir Watkin Williams Wynne, Francis Coke, Henry Jones Williams, and Humphrey Rowland Jones by name. In the Llanerfyl award, two exceeded 10 per cent – Wynne (1603 acres) and Clive (1221 acres).

Notes: JJ 2317. 1826 award covered Llanerfyl, 1829 award covered Llangadfan.

56011   LLANFAIR CAEREINION

Act 50 Geo. III c. 186 1810. Awards 1818, 1819, 1822, 1826.

Grid reference: SJ (33) 104 065.

Common and waste: 7000 acres (Act), 8614 acres (actual).

Caereinion Iscoed. Partly in parishes of Llangynyw and Castle Caereinion.

Commissioner: Valentine Vickers senior of Cranmere, who died and was replaced by Valentine Vickers junior, also of Cranmere.
Surveyor: Charles Mickleburgh of Montgomery, who replaced Thomas Kyffin of Copthorn. Mickleburgh described in award as 'of Copthorn'.

Award: i)   NLW Mont C C 6, 7, 10, 15, 23, 28;   ii) NLW Powis Castle M112, M113, M114, M115.

Principal allottees: Seventeen exceeded 100 acres, including the common owners of the turbary lots (107 acres). Three exceeded 5 per cent — Humphrey Rowland Jones (1400 acres), the late Earl of Powis (1160 acres) and Sir Watkin Williams Wynn (1143 acres).

Notes: JJ 2270.

56009 LLANFECHAIN

Act 29 Geo. III c. 17 1789. Awards 1798 and 1828.

Grid reference: SJ (33) 189 204.

Open fields, common and waste: 5000 acres (Act), 2152 acres (actual).

Plas Dinas and Mechain Iscoed. Partly in parishes of Llanfihangel-yng-Ngwynfa, Llansanffraid-yn-Mechan, and Meifod.

Commissioners: John Bishton of Kilsall, who completed award of 1798, but was replaced by David Jones of Llanfyllin for 1828. Act also appointed Thomas Matthews of Shelderton, Thomas Lovett of Chirk, and Henry Bowman of Knockin to act as arbitrators if required.

Award: i)   NLW Mont C C 20, 26, 43;   ii)   NLW Powis Castle M92, M93.

Principal allottees: None received 10 per cent. Two exceeded 100 acres — Sir Watkin Williams Wynn (186 acres) and Revd Thomas Trevor Trevor (141 acres).

Notes: JJ 2222.

LLANFIHANGEL-YNG-NGWYNFA
   (i)   See Llanfechain (56009).

   (ii) See Llanfyllin (56012).

LLANFYLLIN

56010 (i) Act 29 Geo. III c. 24 (Public) 1789. Award 1797.

Grid reference: SJ (33) 142 196.

Common and waste: 124 acres (Dodd).

Globwll and Bachau (Bachie).

Commissioner: Thomas Matthews of Shelderton.

Award: i)   NLW Mont C C 44;   ii)   NLW Powis Castle M94.

Principal allottees: Most of the land was sold, the major buyers being the heirs of Bell Lloyd (58 acres), and John Humphreys (24 acres).

Notes: JJ not listed. The extant copy is now illegible in places. The enclosure was to raise money to cover the costs of repairing the market house at Llanfyllin.

56012 (ii) Act 51 Geo. III c. 87 1811. Awards 1819 and 1826.

Grid reference: SJ (33) 142 196.

Open field, common and waste: 4495 acres (Act), 3531 acres (actual).

Brynelltyn, Garthgell, Bodfach Cammen and others, in Llanfyllin and Mechain Uwchcoed manors. Township of Bodyddon. Partly in parishes of Meifod and Llanfihangel-yng-Ngwynfa.

Commissioners: Valentine Vickers senior of Cranmere, who resigned and was replaced by Henry Bowman of Knockin. Dodd also records Thomas Kyffin and H. Browne, and Jones (1879) gives Henry Browne as the sole commissioner mentioned in the Act. There is no evidence that Browne ever acted, while Kyffin was originally surveyor, but replaced Bowman for final award of 1826.

Award: i)   NLW Mont C C 22 (1819 award) and photocopy Powis Castle copy (1826 award);   ii) NLW Powis Castle M117, M119 (1826 award);   iii) CRO M/QS/DE/1 (1819 award).

Principal allottees: Two exceeded 10 per cent – Sir Watkin Williams Wynn (1226 acres) and the Earl of Powis (404 acres).

Notes: JJ 2275. 1819 award covered Mechain Uwchcoed, 1826 Llanfyllin.

LLANGADFAN   See Llanerfyl (56008).

LLANGURIG

56013 (i) Order 1855. Award 1857.
Provisional Order of 27 July 1854, confirmed by 18-19 Vic. c. 61.

Grid reference: SN (22) 960 825.

Common and waste: 91 acres (award), 89 acres (actual).

Bryn Postig Hill.

Valuer: David Davies of Froodvale.

Award: i) PRO (Kew) MAF 1/706; ii) NLW Mont C C 45.

Principal allottees: Three exceeded 10 per cent - George Brace (32 acres), Ann Warburton Owen (20) and John Davies (9).

Notes: JJ 2356. JJ apparently confuses this with 56014.

56014 (ii) Order 1856. Award 1860.
Provisional Order of 3 April 1856, confirmed by 19-20 Vic. c. 106.

Grid reference: SN (22) 931 815.

Common and waste: 230 acres (actual).

Wauntwrch, Blaenpathnog (Blaenpathiog) and Clap Llanerch, in townships of Glyngynwidd and Glynbrochan.

Valuer: David Davies of Froodvale.

Award: i) PRO (Kew) MAF 1/805; ii) NLW Mont C C 16.

Principal allottees: Two exceeded 10 per cent - Thomas Edmund Marsh (99 acres) and Mary Matthews (43 acres).

Notes: JJ 2359. There appears to be some confusion in the MAF index between this enclosure and Hyssington (56007).

LLANGWYNYW (LLANGYNYW) See Llanfair Caereinion (56011).

56015   LLANIDLOES

Act 56 Geo. III c. 37 1816. Awards 1826 and 1828.

Grid reference: SN (22) 955 845.

Common and waste: Area not stated. Jones (1985) gives a total of 13,236 acres for twenty of the twenty-seven townships involved; an overall total of about 20,000 acres seems probable.

Arustley (Arwystli). Partly in parishes of Llandinam, Llanwnnog, Llysin, Trefeglwys, Penstrywaid, and Carno.

Commissioner: William Pugh of Caer Howell, Francis Souper Bayley, and Frederick Adair Roe were named in the Act, but all refused. John Humphreys of Tyn-y-coed, John Matthews of Mold and George Nuttall of Leominster replaced them, but Nuttall died and was replaced by John Dyer of Cefngwifed. John Maughan of Barnt Green was elected, but removed after court action.
Surveyors: William Humphreys of Berriew; William Jones of Llanidloes; Robert A. Piercy of Llanidloes. (See Jones (1985) for full details of the complex manoeuvrings involved.)

Award: i)   NLW Mont C C 48, 49, 51;   ii)   NLW Chancellor Parry Llandinam Dep vol. 1, 2.

Principal allottees: Act records Sir Watkin Williams Wynn, University College, Oxford, Sir Edward Pryce Lloyd, Sir A. Davies Owen, and twelve others by name.

Papers: Maps of pre-enclosure holdings in Llanwnog exist in NLW Llanwnog Parish Deposits 1-8.

Notes: JJ 2318.

56016   LLANLLUGAN

Order 1853. Award 1862.
Provisional Order of 7 May 1852, confirmed by 16-17 Vic. c. 3.

Grid reference: SJ (33) 058 024.

Common and waste: 1280 acres (actual).

Partly in parish of Castle Caereinion.

Valuer: William Parry of Morfodion in Llanidloes, who died and was replaced by Edward Powell Parry, also of Morfodion. Parry in turn resigned, and was replaced by David Davies of Froodvale.

Award: i) PRO (Kew) MAF 1/230 (map) and /1117 (award); ii) NLW Mont C C 2, and 17.

Principal allottees: Two exceeded 10 per cent – Revd John Arthur Herbert (583 acres) and Harvey Bowen Jones (211 acres).

Notes: JJ 2352.

LLANLLWCHAEARN   See Aberhafesb (56001).

LLANMEREWIG (LLAMYREWIG)   See Aberhafesb (56001).

LLANSANFFRAID   See Llanfechain (56009).

LLANWNNOG   See Llanidloes (56015).

LLANWYDDELAN   See Aberhafesb (56001).

LLYSIN   See Llanidloes (56015).

MANAFON   See Aberhafesb (56001).

MEIFOD
(i) See Guilsfield (56005)

(ii) See Llanfechain (56009)

(iii) See Llanfyllin (56012)

56017 MOCHDRE

Act 37 Geo. III c. 115 1797. Awards 1800, 1803, 1804.

Grid reference: SO (32) 073 886.

Common and waste: 20,000 acres (Act), 10,096 acres (actual).

Kerry Hills. Partly in Kerry parish.

Commissioner: Valentine Vickers junior of Cranmere. Act appointed Henry Bowman of Knockin and Thomas Colley of Cefngwifed as arbitrators, if needed.

Award: i) NLW Mont C C 14; ii) NLW Mont C C 9 (boundary award and map); iii) NLW Powis Castle M108, M109, M110.

Principal allottees: Two exceeded 10 per cent - John Herbert (1916 acres) and Robert Knight (1050 acres).

Notes: JJ 2233.

NEW CHAPEL   See Guilsfield (56005).

NEWTOWN (Y DRENEWYDD)   See Aberhafesb (56001).

PENSTRYWAID (PENSTROWED)   See Llanidloes (56015).

TREFEGLWYS   See Llanidloes (56015).

WELSHPOOL (Y TRALLWNG)

56018 (i)   Act 51 Geo. III c. 89 1811. Award 1812,1816.

Grid reference: SJ (33) 232 085.

Open field, common and waste: 1200 acres (Act), 1413 acres (actual).

Cofronydd, Gungrog Fawr, Tre-wern, Cletterwood, in manor of Teirtref. NLW gives Tre-wern parish.

Commissioner: Valentine Vickers junior of Cranmere, who was replaced by William Wyley of Admaston. Surveyor: Thomas Kyffin.

Award: NLW Powis Castle M116.

Principal allottees: The extant copy is illegible in places. The Earl of Powis was a major owner, with 300 acres.

Notes: JJ 2276.

56019 (ii)   Act 1 Geo. III c. 36 1760. Award ?

Grid reference: SJ (33) 213 076.

Common and waste: 156 acres (Act).

Pool Common or Gwern y go, in hamlets of Llanerchidol and Stret Marcel (Street Marshall or Ystrad Marchell). Partly in Guilsfield parish.

Commissioners: Thomas Lloyd of Trefnant; Henry Wynn of Doleardden; Thomas Brown of Mellington; Jonathan Lloyd of Trefcoed; Devereux Mytton of Guilsfield. Dodd notes that all were local proprietors.

Award: Possibly none made. The Act specified the proportions to go to each owner.

Principal allottees: Act specifies one tenth to the Earl of Powis and nine tenths to the Borough of Pool.

Notes: JJ 2212. NLW Mont C C 27 contains an agreement enclosure for Pool Common (agreement 1807, award 1810, by Thomas Jones of Penbryn).

(iii)   See Churchstoke (56004).

(iv)   See Guilsfield (56005).

PEMBROKESHIRE

57001 CASTLEMARTIN (CASTELLMARTIN)

Act 28 Geo. III c. 30 1788. Award 1788.

Grid reference: SR (11) 911 989.

Common and waste: 274 acres (award), 206 acres ('measured').

Castle Martin Corse.

Commissioners: John Hand of Stackpole Court; David Paynter of Pembroke. Act lists also James Linton of Loveston.

Award: CRO D/ANGLE/121 (preamble only).

Principal allottees: Act records John Campbell, John Hooke Campbell, John Lort, David Rice, John Mirehouse, John Philipps Adams, Benjamin Saunders, James Protheroe, Joseph Nicholas, John Moody, and John Freeman.

Notes: JJ 2220.

57005 CRUNWEAR

Order 1856. Award 1868.
Provisional order of 17 January 1856, confirmed by 19-20 Vic. c. 11.

Grid reference: SN (22) 181 104.

Common and waste: 186 acres (order and actual).

Llanteague Common.

Valuer: William Goode of St Clears, who died and was replaced by Lewis Wilson of Langdon in Begelly.

Award: i) PRO (Kew) MAF 1/744; ii) CRO QRE/8.

Principal allottees: Four exceeded 10 per cent - Thomas Lewis (50 acres), Revd J. H. A. Phillips (40 acres), the trustees of the Picton estate (33 acres), and John H. Scourfield (26 acres).

Notes: JJ 2358.

57009 HAVERFORDWEST (HWLFFORDD)

Act 1-2 Vic. c. 95 (L and P) 1838. Award 1840.

Grid reference: SM (12) 920 155.

Common and waste: 600 acres (Act), 575 acres (award).

Portfield.

Commissioner: John Wilson.
Surveyors: Henry Phelps Goode; Henry Philpott.

Award: i) CRO QRE/7; ii) NLW Room 149 (photocopy of map, with key).

Principal allottees: The Freemen of Haverfordwest received 251 acres, and the Borough 175 acres.

Notes: JJ 2332.

57002 LETTERSTON (TRELETERT)

Order 1856. Award 1864.
Provisional order of 17 April 1856, confirmed by 19-20 Vic. c. 106.

Grid reference: SM (12) 939 297.

Common and waste: 260 acres (order and actual).

Letterston Common.

Valuer: Harry Phelps Goode of Haverfordwest.

Award: i) PRO (Kew) MAF 1/343; ii) CRO QRE/9; iii) NLW Room A 95.

Principal allottees: Two exceeded 50 acres - the Bishop of St Davids (74 acres) and Lewis Mathias (69 acres).

Notes: JJ 2359.

57003 LLANDEILO (LLANDILO)

Act 55 Geo. III c. 92 (not printed) 1815. Award 1820.

Grid reference: SN (22) 105 271.

Common and waste: area not stated.

Partly in parishes of Llangolman and Maenclochog.

Commissioner: Thomas Eaton of Laugharne, and later of Haverfordwest.
Surveyors: James Goode of Haverfordwest; John Hand of Stackpool Court; John Tamlyn of Haverfordwest.

Award: i)   NLW;   ii) CRO MF 207 (microfilm copy).

Principal allottees: Act records Richard, Lord Milford, Richard Le Hunte, Sir John Owen, Joseph Foster Barham and John Philipps Laugharne.

Notes: JJ 2316. Possibly the area refered to in BoA (vol. 2, p.86) of 2500 acres.

57004   LLANFYRNACH

Act 49 Geo. III c. 49 (not printed) 1809. Award 1812.

Grid reference: SN (22) 220 313.

Common and waste: 3000 acres (Act).

Commissioners: Charles Hassall of Eastwood; Thomas Hassall of Kilrhue; Richard Jones of Pantirrion.
Surveyor: William Couling of Carmarthen.

Award: CRO HSPC/5/1.

Principal allottees: Act records Thomas Lloyd and William, Baron Kensington.

Notes: JJ 2266.

LLANGOLMAN   See Llandeilo (57003).

LLAN-TEG   See Crunwear (57005).

LLANWNDA

Order 1911. Award 1912.

Grid reference: SM (12) 943 380.

Common and waste: 1.1 acres (award).

Goodwick Common.

RADNORSHIRE

Valuer: None.

Award: PRO (Kew) MAF 25/41/B1615.

Principal allottees: Land taken for a replacement church, with £1 compensation to commoners.

Notes: Not in JJ. Not counted here, though in reality it is little different to e.g. the Portsea (1735) enclosure listed by Turner.

MAENCLOCHOG   See Llandeilo (57003).

57006 MANOROWEN

Act 2-3 Wm IV c. 35 (not printed) 1832. Award 1833.

Grid reference: SM (12) 934 364.

Common and waste: 150 acres (Act), 101 acres ('measured').

Commissioner: John Harvey of Haverfordwest.
Surveyor: Henry Phelps Goode of Haverfordwest.

Award: CRO QRE/6.

Principal allottees: Act records Richard Bowen, Gwynne Gill Vaughan, and Thomas Mathias.

Notes: JJ 2329.

57007 MARLOES

Act 51 Geo. III c. 10 (not printed) 1811. Award 1814.

Grid reference: SM (12) 793 086.

Common and waste: 163 acres (Act), 300 acres (BoA).

Commissioner: John Hand of Stackpool Court.

Award: CRO QRE/4.

Principal allottees: Act records only William, Baron Kensington.

Notes: JJ 2285.

MOLLESTON   See Narberth (57008).

MONACHLOGDDU (MYNACHLOG-DDU)

Order 1898. Award 1899.

Grid reference: SN (22) 131 282.

Common and waste: 8.5 acres (award).

Waun Isaf Common.

Valuer: None.

Award: PRO(Kew) MAF 25/41/B3776.

Principal allottees: Land released to Lords of Manor of Monachlogddu in exchange for other land given up.

Notes: Not in JJ. May perhaps be regarded technically as an enclosure, though not counted here.

57008   NARBERTH

Act   26 Geo. III c. 14 1786. Award ?

Grid reference: SN (22) 108 145.

Common and waste: 2450 acres (Act), 1826 acres (BoA).

Narberth Forest, with Templeton Mountain, Molleston Mountain, and Robeston Grove, in townships of Templeton, Molleston, and Robeston. Partly in Robeston Wathan parish.

Commissioners: Revd William Evans of Llawhaden; Stephen Griffiths of Langolman; George Phelps of Studda; Nicholas Roch of Paskeston.
Surveyor: Charles Hassall of Eastwood.

Award: Not known.

Principal allottees: Act records William Knox, Richard, Baron Milford, and William, Baron Kensington. BoA says Lord received 500 acres.

Notes: JJ 2218. NLW Slebech 3775 contains copy of part of award, NLW Picton contains more. No date given for award, but before 21 September 1798.

PORTFIELD   See Haverfordwest (57009).

ROBESTON WATHAN   See Narberth (57008).

57010 ST DAVID'S (TYDDEWI)

Order 1863.   Award 1869.
Provisional order of 20 November 1862, confirmed by 26-27 Vic. c. 18.

Grid reference: SM (12) 751 255.

Common and waste: 212 acres (actual).

Manor of Dewsland.

Valuer: Thomas Tamlyn of Haverfordwest.
Surveyor: Henry Philpott of Haverfordwest.

Award: i)   PRO (Kew) MAF 1/529;   ii)   CRO QRE/10.
iii) NLW Photocopy.

Principal allottees: Only three exceeded 10 acres - Ebenezer Rees (94 acres), William Rees (70 acres), and the Bishop of St Davids (31 acres).

Notes: JJ 2372.

TEMPLETON   See Narberth (57008).

RADNORSHIRE

ABBEYCWMHIR (ABATY CWM-HIR)   See Llanbadarn Fynydd (58016).

58001 BEGUILDY (BUGEILDY)

(i) Order 1849. Award 1857.
Provisional Order of 8 February 1849, confirmed by 12-13 Vic. c. 57.

Grid reference: SO (32) 195 797.

Common and waste: 2193 acres (order), 2192 acres (actual).

Creig Byther in South Ugre manor.

Valuer: William Eyton of Gonsal in Condover.

Award: i)   PRO (Kew) MAF 1/76;   ii)   PRO (Chancery) LRRO 1/67 and MR 857;   iii) PRO (Chancery) CREST 6/179 A;   iv)   CRO R/QS/DE/12.

Principal allottees: Three exceeded 200 acres - George Stansal Griffiths (390 acres), William Matthews (260 acres), and James Meredith (213 acres).

Notes: JJ 2347.

(ii)   See Heyope (58014).

58002 BETWS DISERTH

Order 1882. Award 1885.
Provisional Order of 28 January 1880, confirmed by 45-46 Vic. c. 29.

Grid reference: SO (32) 110 578.

Common and waste: 1988 acres (order), 685 acres (actual).

Cefn Drawen.

Valuer: Stephen William Williams of Rhayader.

Award: i)   PRO (Kew) MAF 1/454;   ii)   CRO R/QS/DE/5.

Principal allottees: Four exceeded 50 acres – Cecil Joseph Parsons (205 acres), Mrs Matilda Bedward (134 acres), Edwin Davies (61 acres), and Sir Joseph R Bailey (50 acres).

Notes: JJ 2386.

58003 BLEDDFA

Act 7-8 Vic. c. 8 1844. Award 1853 (2).

Grid reference: SO (32) 207 683.

Common and waste: 5000 acres (Act).

Forest Fach and Starling Bank in the manors of Bleddfa and South Rurallt. Partly in Llangynllo parish.

Commissioner: William Eyton of Gonsal in Condover.

Award: i) CRO R/QS/DE/30; ii) PRO (Chancery) LRRO 1/3649-3654 (plans).

Principal allottees: Act records Richard Price, Sir John Walsh, and John Weyman.

Notes: JJ 2338. Two awards in same year.

58004 BOUGHROOD (BOCHRWYD)

Order 1860. Award 1867.
Provisional Order of 22 December 1859, confirmed by 23-24 Vic. c. 17.

Grid reference: SO (32) 128 394.

Common and waste: 702 acres (order), 701 acres (actual).

Llanwimp and Llansteffan Commons. Partly in Llansteffan parish.

Valuer: David Brown of Brecon.

Award: i) PRO (Kew) MAF 1/211 (map) and 1/914 (award); ii) CRO R/QS/DE/8.

Principal allottees: Only one exceeded 10 per cent, Walter De Winton (389 acres).

Notes: JJ 2366.

58005   CASGOB

    Act   53 Geo. III c. 150 1813. Award 1816.

    Grid reference: SO (32) 224 659.

    Common and waste: 1500 acres (Act).

    In townships of Ednol and Kinnerton.

    Commissioners: John Cheese of Lyonshall; James Stephens of Presteigne. The latter was also Assistant Commissioner.

    Award: i) CRO R/QS/DE/9; ii) PRO (Chancery) LRRO 1/3676 (certified copy of plan).

    Principal allottees: Act records the King, Samuel Lewin, Thomas Stephens, and John Whittaker.

    Papers: PRO (Chancery) CREST 6/123 and 6/145.

    Notes: JJ 2304.

CEFN-LLYS

58006 (i)   Order 1865. Award 1869.
    Provisional Order of 6 May 1865, confirmed by 28-29 Vic. c. 39.

    Grid reference: SO (32) 085 615.

    Common and waste: 112 acres (order), 111 acres (actual).

    Cefnllys Commons.

    Valuer: George Owen of Oswestry.

    Award: i) PRO (Kew) MAF 1/590; ii) CRO R/QS/DE/10.

    Principal allottees: Lord Ormathwaite received 97 acres.

    Notes: JJ 2378.

58007 (ii) Order 1880. Award 1885.
    Provisional Order of 28 January 1880, confirmed by 43-44 Vic. c. 87.

    Grid reference: SO (32) 085 615.

Common and waste: 128 acres (order and actual).

Hendy Bank.

Valuer: Stephen William Williams of Rhayader.

Award: i) PRO (Kew) MAF 1/924; ii) CRO R/QS/DE/16.

Principal allottees: Three exceeded 10 per cent – the late Thomas Vaughan (63 acres), Boughrood Charity (37 acres) and Evan Powell Welson (20 acres).

Notes: JJ 2384.

58008 CLYRO (CLEIRWY)

Act 53 Geo. III c. 143 1813. Award ?

Grid reference: SO (32) 213 439.

Common and waste: 2000 acres (Act).

Commissioners: John Cheese of Lyonshall; James Stephens of Presteigne.

Award: Not known.

Principal allottees: Act records Walter Wilkins, William Davies, James Beavan, Samuel Lewin, Revd Richard Venables, and Bishop of St Davids.

Papers: Text of Act in CRO RC/E/CLY/3/41-42.

Notes: JJ 2302.

COLVA (COLFA) See Gladestry (58012).

DISCOED HILL See Presteigne (58009).

58010 DISERTH

Act 52 Geo. III c. 64 1812. Award ?

Grid reference: SO (32) 034 583.

Common and waste: 920 acres (Act), 1600 acres (BoA).

Manors of Upper Elvell and Llechryd. Partly in
Llanelwedd parish. BoA says 1100 acres (Diserth),
500 acres (Llanelwedd).

Commissioners: John Cheese of Lyonshall; James
Stephens of Presteigne.

Award: Not known.

Principal allottees: Act records the late Revd
Richard Powell, Thomas Thomas, David Thomas,
Marmaduke Howell, and Thomas Gwynne.

Notes: JJ 2289. He also lists under 2296, with same
Chapter number, but not printed.

EDNOL   See Casgob (58005).

58011   EVENJOBB

Order 1847.   Award 1849.
Provisional Order of 25 August 1846, confirmed by
10-11 Vic. c. 25.

Grid reference: SO (32) 262 623.

Common and waste: 259 acres (order), 297 acres
(actual).

Evenjobb Hill.

Valuer: Edward Morris Sayce of Kington.

Award: i)   PRO (Kew) MAF 1/713;   ii) CRO
R/QS/DE/14.

Principal allottees: Two exceeded 10 per cent –
Peter Rickards Mynors (195 acres) and the Earl of
Oxford and Mortimer (30 acres).

Notes: JJ 2341. Also recorded as Old Radnor.

58012   GLADESTRY (LLANFAIR LLYTHYNWG)

Act   50 Geo. III c. 116 1810.   Award 1813.

Grid reference: SO (32) 231 551.

Common and waste: 960 acres (Act and actual). Award
specifies total 928 acres, listed as 540 acres in
Gladestry and 388 acres in Colva.

Huntington Hill.

Commissioners: John Cheese of Lyonshall; James Stephens of Presteigne.

Award: i) CRO R/QS/DE/15; ii) PRO (Chancery) LRRO 1/3664 (plan, copy).

Principal allottees: Five exceeded 50 acres - Rev. Benjamin Jones (102 acres), James Watt (98 acres), the representatives of Edmund Cheese (92 acres), Thomas Lewis (75 acres), and Thomas Trumper (74).

Papers: PRO (Chancery) CREST 6/108.

Notes: JJ 2268.

GLASGWM (GLASCWM)

58013 (i) Order 1882. Award 1885.
Provisional Order of 28 January 1880, confirmed by 45-46 Vic. c. 30.

Grid reference: SO (32) 155 531.

Common and waste: 834 acres (order and actual).

Cefn Drawen, Rhiew, Werndridd.

Valuer: Stephen William Williams of Rhayader.

Award: i) PRO (Kew) MAF 1/455; ii) CRO R/QS/DE/6.

Principal allottees: Two exceeded 10 per cent - Sir Joseph Russell Bailey (98 acres) and William Williams Thomas Moore (84 acres).

Notes: JJ 2387.

58019 (ii) Order 1880. Award 1885.
Provisional Order of 28 January 1880, confirmed by 43-44 Vic. c. 89.

Grid reference: SO (32) 135 590.

Common and waste: 340 acres (order), 341 acres (actual).

Llandegley Rhos Common.

Valuer: Stephen William Williams of Rhayader.

Award: PRO (Kew) MAF 1/528.

Principal allottees: Four exceeded 10 per cent – Evan Powell Welson (102 acres), Eliza Davies (75 acres), Boughrood Charity (45 acres), and the late Thomas Lewis Vaughan (36 acres).

Notes: JJ 2385. The award specifies that it refers to that part of the common lying in Glasgwm parish.

58014 HEYOPE

Order 1868. Award 1873.
Provisional Order of 10 July 1867, confirmed by 31-32 Vic. c. 31.

Grid reference: SO (32) 251 742.

Common and waste: 1,120 acres (award), 1107 (actual).

Manors of Knucklas and South Ugre (Swydd Beddugre). Partly in parishes of Beguildy and Llangyllo.

Valuer: John Mickleburgh of Montgomery.

Award: i) PRO (Kew) MAF 1/375 (map) and /1076 (award); ii) CRO R/QS/DE/17; iii) PRO (Chancery) LRRO 1/3687 (plans).

Principal allottees: Two exceeded 100 acres – William Heaford Daubney (115 acres) and Thomas Tudge (107 acres).

Notes: JJ 2381.

ISCOED   See Nantmel (58025).

KINNERTON   See Casgob (58005).

KNIGHTON (TREFYCLO)

58015 (i) Act 7-8 Vic. c. 6 1844. Award 1848.

Grid reference: SO (32) 263 719.

Common and waste: 800 acres (Act).

Cwmgilla and Farrington manors.

Commissioner: William Eyton of Gonsal in Condover.

Award: i) CRO R/QS/DE/28; ii) PRO (Chancery) LRRO 1/3678 and 1/3674 (certified copies of plan).

Principal allottees: Act records Edward Rogers, Venerable Archdeacon Vickers, and Richard Price.

Notes: JJ 2337.

58017 (ii) Order 1853. Award 1859.
Provisional Order of 5 January 1853, confirmed by 16-17 Vic. c. 120.

Grid reference: SO (32) 287 725.

Common and waste: 72 acres (order), 71 acres (actual).

Knighton manor.

Valuer: William Eyton of Gonsal in Condover.

Award: i) PRO (Kew) MAF 1/707; ii) PRO (Chancery) LRRO 1/27 and MPE 127.

Principal allottees: Only two exceeded 10 acres – Robert Henry Price (23 acres) and Thomas Jones (13 acres).

Papers: PRO (Chancery) CREST 6/179 A.

Notes: JJ 2353.

KNUCKLAS   See Heyope (58014).

LLANANNO   See Llanbadarn Fynydd (58016).

LLANBADARN FAWR   See Llandrindod (58020).

58016 LLANBADARN FYNYDD

Act 9-10 Vic. c. 5 1846. Award 1857.

Grid reference: SO (32) 098 777.

Common and waste: 7000 acres (Act).

Manor of Gollen (Golon). Partly in parishes of Llananno, Llanbister, Llanddewi Ystradenni, Abbeycwmhir, and St Harmon.

Commissioner: William Eyton of Gonsal in Condover.
Surveyor: Charles Mickleburgh.

Award: CRO R/QS/DE/2/1-3.

Principal allottees: Act records John Cheesement Severn, Francis Philips, and Jonathon Field.

Papers: Objections in CRO R/D/BRA/1862/57.

Notes: JJ 2340.

LLANBISTER   See Llanbadarn Fynydd (58016).

58020 LLANDRINDOD

Order 1862.   Award 1870.
Provisional Order of 15 May 1862, confirmed by 25-26 Vic. c. 94.

Grid reference: SO (32) 058 610.

Common and waste: 3220 acres (order), 2026 acres (actual).

Swydd Neithon (Dinieithon) manor in the townships of Llandrindod, Cefnllys, Llanbadarn Fawr, Maestyr-Rhos- Llanddu, and Swydd and Graig. Partly in the parishes of Cefn-llys, Llanddewi Ystradenni, Llandegley, and Llanbadarn Fawr.

Valuer: John Mickleburgh of Montgomery.

Award: (i) PRO (Kew) MAF 1/512 (map) and 1/1015 (award);   (ii) PRO (Chancery) LRRO 1/3682, 1/3683, 1/3685.   (iii) CRO R/QS/DE/1.

Principal allottees: Two exceeded 10 per cent - Lord Ormathwaite (444 acres) and James W. G. Watt (354 acres).

Notes: JJ 2370.

LLANDDEWI YSTRADENNI

58018 (i) Order 1860. Award 1862.
Provisional Order of 7 June 1860, confirmed by 23-24 Vic. c. 55.

Grid reference: SO (32) 108 686.

Common and waste: 614 acres (order and actual).

Rhosliswal, Latch Rhos, and Melenydd, in the township of Church Llanddewi, and manor of Ugre.

Valuer: George Owen of Oswestry.

Award: i) PRO (Kew) MAF 1/329; ii) PRO (Chancery) MR 618 (removed from LRRO 1/46).

Principal allottees: Sir John Benn Welsh received over 90 per cent (553 acres).

Notes: JJ 2367.

(ii)   See Llanbadarn Fynydd (58016).

(iii) See Llandrindod (58020).

LLANELWEDD (LLANELWETH)   See Diserth (58010).

LLANFIHANGEL HELYGEN

58023 (i) Act 3-4 Vic. c. 16 1840. Award 1843.

Grid reference: SO (32) 045 644.

Common and waste: 195 acres (award).

Manors of Ywchcoed, Iscoed, Rhysllyn. Partly in parishes of St Harmon, Nantmel, and Llanyre.

Commissioners: Josiah Castree of Gloucester; John Iveson of Halliford. Act appointed Charles Mickleburgh as Umpire, if required.

Award: i) CRO R/QS/DE/7; ii) PRO (Chancery) LRRO 1/3665 (plan), 1/3666 and 1/3679-3681.

Principal allottees: Act records James Watt and Venerable Richard Venables.

Notes: JJ 2335.

(ii)   See Nantmel (58025).

58022   LLANFIHANGEL NANTMELAN

Act 52 Geo. III c. 42 1812. Award 1820.

Grid reference: SO (32) 180 582.

Common and waste: 2156 acres (award).

Manors of Llanwenny and Radnor Foreign.

Commissioners: John Cheese of Lyonshall; James Stephens of Presteigne.

Award: CRO R/QS/DE/21.

Principal allottees: Act records Thomas Frankland Lewis, Edward Burton, and Borough of New Radnor.

Notes: JJ 2287.

58021   LLANFIHANGEL RHYDIEITHON

Order 1861. Award 1864.
Provisional Order of 7 February 1861, confirmed by 24-25 Vic. c. 38.

Grid reference: SO (32) 151 667.

Common and waste: 2810 acres (order), 2823 acres (actual).

Valuer: John Mickleburgh of Montgomery.

Award: i) PRO (Kew) MAF 1/74 (map) and 1/858 (award); ii) CRO R/QS/DE/22; iii) NLW Parish deposit; iv) PRO (Chancery) LRRO 1/3714 and 1/3715

Principal allottees: Two exceeded 10 per cent - Thomas Moore (752 acres) and Sir John Walsh (672 acres).

Notes: JJ 2368.

LLANGYNLLO
(i)   See Bleddfa (58003).

(ii) See Heyope (58004).

LLANSTEFFAN   See Boughrood (58014).

LLANYRE (LLANLLŶR) See Llanfihangel Helygen (58023).

NANTMEL

58024 (i) Order 1863. Award 1871.
Provisional Order of 1 January 1863, confirmed by 26-27 Vic. c. 39.

Grid reference: SO (32) 034 663.

Common and waste: 2810 acres (order), 4068 acres (actual).

Ywchcoed manor. Partly in St Harmon parish.

Valuer: Stephen William Williams of Rhayader.

Award: i) PRO (Kew) MAF 1/249 (map) and 1/1075 (award); ii) CRO R/QS/DE/3; iii) PRO (Chancery) LRRO 1/3716 and 1/3717.

Principal allottees: Two exceeded 300 acres – Colonel John and Mrs Ann Sladen (425 acres) and James W. G. Watt (371 acres)

Notes: JJ 2373.

58025 (ii) Order 1862. Award 1867.
Provisional Order of 15 May 1862, confirmed by 25-26 Vic. c. 94.

Grid reference: SO (32) 034 663.

Common and waste: 687 acres (order), 690 acres (actual).

Iscoed manor. Partly in Llanfihangel Helygen parish.

Valuer: Stephen William Williams of Rhayader.

Award: i) PRO (Kew) MAF 1/305 (map) and 1/918 (award); ii) CRO R/QS/DE/18; iii) PRO (Chancery) LRRO 1/3719.

Principal allottees: Only one exceeded 10 per cent, Thomas Williams Higgins (140 acres).

Notes: JJ 2370.

58032   (iii)   Order 1863.   Award 1870.
Provisional Order of 1 January 1863, confirmed by 26-27 Vic. c. 39.

Grid reference: SO (32) 034 663.

Common and waste: 2850 acres (order), 2852 acres (actual).

Manor of Rhysllyn.

Valuer: Stephen William Williams of Rhayader.

Award: i)   PRO (Kew) MAF 1/351 (map) and 1/1069 (award);   ii)   CRO R/QS/DE/27;   iii) PRO (Chancery) LRRO 1/3713.

Principal allottees: Two exceeded 10 per cent - William Davies (354 acres) and James W. G. Watt (313 acres).

Notes: JJ 2373.

(iv)   See Llanfihangel Helygen (58023).

58027 NORTON

Order 1864.   Award 1867.
Provisional Order of 22 December 1863, confirmed by 27-28 Vic. c. 1.

Grid reference: SO (32) 304 673.

Common and waste: 720 acres (order), 705 acres (actual).

Valuer: John Mickleburgh of Montgomery.

Award: i)   PRO (Kew) MAF 1/312 (map) and 927 (award);   ii)   CRO R/QS/DE/4.

Principal allottees: Only one exceeded 10 per cent, Richard Green Price (538 acres).

Notes: JJ 2374. He also lists a second Norton enclosure, with a Provisional Order of 28 April 1864, confirmed by 27-28 Vic. c. 66 (2376). This appears to be the one listed here under Whitton (58034).

58026 PILLETH (PYLLALAI)

Act 52 Geo. III c. 44 1812 Award ?

Grid reference: SO (32) 256 682.

Common and waste: Area not stated. 800 acres (BoA).

Pilleth Hill in lordship of Cantremellenith.

Commissioners: John Cheese of Lyonshall; James Stephens of Presteigne.

Award: None known. PRO (Chancery) LRRO 1/3675 contains a certified tracing of the map.

Principal allottees: Act records the King, Richard Price, Thomas Frankland Lewis, and Edward Jenkins.

Notes: JJ 2288.

58009 PRESTEIGNE (LLANANDRAS)

Order 1848. Award 1851.
Provisional Order of 24 May 1848, confirmed by 11-12 Vic. c. 109.

Grid reference: SO (32) 315 645.

Common and waste: 92 acres (award and actual).

Discoed Hill.

Valuer: Edward Morris Sayce of Kington.

Award: i) PRO (Kew) MAF 1/629; ii) CRO R/QS/DE/13.

Principal allottees: Three exceeded 10 per cent - Arthur Partridge (43 acres), Joseph Middleton (23 acres), and John Adcock Phillips (12 acres).

Papers: PRO (Chancery) CREST 6/179 A.

Notes: JJ 2344.

58028 RADNOR FOREST (CLUD)

Order 1861. Award 1867.
Provisional Order of 14 March 1861, confirmed by 24-25 Vic. c. 38.

Grid reference: SO (32) 182 639.

Common and waste: 4420 acres (order), 4413 acres (actual).

Valuer: John Tench of Ludlow.

Award: i) PRO (Kew) MAF 1/90 (map) and 1/915 (award); ii) CRO R/QS/DE/26.

Principal allottees: Two exceeded 10 per cent – Revd Sir Gilbert Frankland Lewis (2072 acres), and R. P. B. and P. R. Mynors (472 acres).

Notes: JJ 2368.

58029 RADNOR, NEW (MAESYFED)

Act 51 Geo. III c. 161 1811. Award 1814.

Grid reference: SO (32) 212 608.

Common and waste: 1624 acres (Act), 1552 acres (actual).

Smatcher Hill, Knowle Hill, Fron Hill, Monyrythen, Cwmynace Hill, Habbatch Hill, Himble (Wimble) Hill, Cwym Bailey Glase.

Commissioners: John Cheese of Lyonshall; James Stephens of Presteigne.
Surveyor: Maurice Sayce.

Award: i) CRO R/QS/DE/23;   ii) NLW Harpton 4 (map only).

Principal allottees: Three exceeded 5 per cent – Thomas Frankland Lewis (594 acres), Percival Lewis (420 acres), and Samuel Lewin (98 acres).

Notes: JJ 2281.

RADNOR, OLD (PENCRAIG)

58031 (i) Order 1868. Award 1870.
Provisional Order of 2 April 1868, confirmed by 31–32 Vic. c. 82.

Grid reference: SO (32) 222 588.

Common and waste: 349 acres (order), 352 acres (actual).

Harpton and Wolfpitts.

Valuer: Stephen William Williams of Rhayader.

Award: i) PRO (Kew) MAF 1/756; ii) NLW Harpton 1; iii) CRO R/QS/DE/24.

Principal allottees: One received 89 per cent, Revd Sir Gilbert Frankland Lewis (314 acres).

Papers: Valuer's papers, plan and report in CRO R/D/WWA/1/798.

Notes: JJ 2382.

(ii)   See Evenjobb (58011).

58030 RHAYADER (RHAEADR GWY)

Act 9 Geo. IV c. 48 (not printed) 1828. Award 1829.

Grid reference: SN (22) 969 681.

Common and waste: 80 acres (Act), 76 acres (actual).

Manor and borough of Rhayader.

Commissioner: Morris Sayce of Kington.
Surveyor: William Sayce of Kington.

Award: i) PRO (Chancery) LRRO 1/3620; ii) PRO (Chancery) CREST 6/179 C; iii) CRO R/D/WWA/1/62 (copy of award and town lots); iv) CRO R/D/WWA/1/794-6 (extract plan of 1898).

Principal allottees: Only two received 10 per cent - Thomas Lewis Lloyd (8 acres) and Hugh Powell Evans (8 acres).

Notes: JJ 2326.

RHYSLLYN
(i)   See Nantmel (58032).

(ii)   See Llanfihangel Helygen (58023).

SOUTH RURALLT   See Bleddfa (58003).

ST HARMON

58033 (i) Order 1849. Award 1860.
Provisional Order of 5 January 1849, confirmed by 12-13 Vic. c. 57.

Grid reference: SN (22) 989 728.

Common and waste: 2890 acres (order and actual).

Glasgarmon (Clasgarmon).

Valuer: Charles Mickleburgh of Montgomery.

Award: i) PRO (Kew) MAF 1/38; ii) NLW Freeman PE 83; iii) PRO (Chancery) LRRO 1/3668 (plan); iv) CRO R/QS/DE/11.

Principal allottees: Two exceeded 10 per cent - James Prickard (713 acres) and David Oliver (418 acres).

Notes: JJ 2347.

(ii)   See Llanbadarn Fynydd (58016).

(iii) See Llanfihangel Helygen (58023).

(iv)   See Nantmel (58024).

UGRE   See Llanddewi Ystradenni (58018).

UGRE, SOUTH
(i)   See Beguildy (58001).

(ii) See Heyope (58014).

58034 WHITTON

Order 1864. Award 1870.
Provisional Order of 28 April 1864, confirmed by 27-28 Vic. c. 60.

Grid reference: SO (32) 272 674.

Common and waste: 728 acres (order and actual).

The Rhos and other lands in the manor of South Rurallt in Whitton.

Valuer: Charles Mickleburgh of Montgomery.

Award: i) PRO (Kew) MAF 1/509; ii) CRO R/PC/6/ENC/1.

Principal allottees: Three exceeded 10 per cent - Richard Green Price (359 acres), Eliza and Edward Jenkins (141 acres), and Edward Coates (118 acres).

Notes: JJ 2376.

YWCHCOED   See Nantmel (58024).

DIRECTORY OF WELSH ENCLOSURE COMMISSIONERS

NOTE: Figures refer to awards as commissioner or valuer, unless otherwise specified. Any additional awards in any other capacity are given in brackets, but these totals are not necessarily fully comprehensive. Counties of residence are omitted where these are the same as the one in which the work was carried out.

ALGEO
Robert
Of Hendy in Llanfair Pwllgwyngyll (to 1864); of Menai Bridge (from 1866).
Active: 1860-1870
Awards: Anglesey 2 (46001, 46008)

ATTREE
Richard
Wakeford
Of Liss, HANTS (to 1855); of Ruabon (Rhiwabon) DENBIGHSHIRE (from 1855). Also had a business address at 8, Cannon Row, Westminster.
Born c.1813. Active: 1848-death 1861
Awards: Anglesey 1 (46004), Cardiganshire 1 (49005), Denbighshire 4 (51003, 51005, 51017, 51024), ENGLAND 9.
Notes: Memorial in Selbourne, HANTS, churchyard says died at Corwen, North Wales.

BAYLEY
Francis Souper
Address not given
Active: 1816
Awards: Montgomeryshire 1 (56015; in fact took no part)

BELL
George
Of Rhyl
Land Surveyor
Active: 1863-1870
Awards: Flint 1 (52012)

BEVAN
William
Of Swansea (Abertawe)
Active: 1833-1835
Awards: Glamorgan 1 (53007)

BISHTON
John senior
Of Kilsall, SHROPSHIRE
Active: 1785-c.1800
Awards: Montgomeryshire 2 (56005, 56009), ENGLAND 11
Notes: Son of same name also active commissioner.

BLATHWAYT Edmund	Address not given Active: 1830-1854 Awards: Carmarthenshire (surveyor 1: 50008)
BOTHAM Samuel	Of Uttoxeter, STAFFORDSHIRE Ironmaster Active: 1800-death 1823 Awards: Montgomeryshire (surveyor 1: 56005), ENGLAND 4
BOWEN John	Of Froodvale (Ffrwd-fâl) (to 1809); of Llansadwrn (1812); of Llandilo Fawr (from 1814). Land Surveyor Active: 1804-1818 Awards: Carmarthenshire 1 (50022) (surveyor 3: 50012, 50013, 50020)
BOWMAN Henry	Of Knockin, SHROPSHIRE Esquire Active: 1785-1826 Awards: Montgomeryshire 2 (56005, 56012) (arbitrator 2: 56009, 56017), ENGLAND 13
BOYDELL James	Of Rossett (Yr Orsedd) (to 1807); of Llay (Llai) (from 1807), both DENBIGHSHIRE Active: 1798-1848 Awards: Denbighshire 1 (51008), Flint (surveyor 1: 52008), ENGLAND 5
BOYDELL Josiah	Of Cilhendre near Ellesmere, SHROPSHIRE (to 1797); of Rossett (Yr Orsedd), DENBIGHSHIRE (from 1797). Also recorded in some later awards as of Cilhendre. Active: 1791-1836 Awards: Denbighshire 2 (51004, 51013) (umpire 1: 51002), Flint 4 (52002, 52008, 52009, 52013), Merionethshire 3 (54002, 54003, 54004), ENGLAND 2 Notes: Listed as a proprietor in Ellesmere award. Nephew of John Boydell, London alderman and engraver, and son of Thomas.
BOYDELL Thomas	Of Trevallyn, DENBIGHSHIRE. Born c.1729. Active: 1775-death 1795 Awards: Flint 2 (52004, 52006), ENGLAND 2
BRIGHT William	Of Admaston, SHROPSHIRE. Active: 1837 (died) Awards: Denbighshire 1 (51021)

BROWN David	Of Brecon (Aberhonddu) Land Surveyor Active: 1860-1867 Awards: Radnorshire 1 (58004)
BROWN(E) Thomas	Of Luton, BEDFORDSHIRE (to 1811); of Brickendon, HERTFORDSHIRE (from 1818). Active: 1800-1820 Awards: Glamorgan 1 (53002), ENGLAND at least 11 Notes: Worked in at least six English counties, but liable to confusion with Thomas Brown of Hitchin, so total activities not clear.
BROWNE Thomas junior	Of Luton, BEDFORDSHIRE Active: 1801-1809 Awards: Glamorgan (surveyor 1: 53002)
BROWN Thomas	Of Mellington near Welshpool Esquire Active: 1761 Awards: Montgomeryshire 1 (56019)
BURD Timotheus	Of Cardiston (to c.1825); of Westbury (from c.1825), both SHROPSHIRE Active: 1808-1827 Awards: Flint 1 (52020), ENGLAND 1
BURTON Francis	Of Aynho, NORTHAMPTONSHIRE Active: 1758-death 1778 Awards: Monmouthshire 1 (55003), ENGLAND 70 Notes: One of the dozen or so most active commissioners in England.
CALVELY James	Of Huntingdon, CHESHIRE Active: 1791-1820 Awards: Flint 1 (52013), ENGLAND 2 Notes: Eden records him as a surveyor in 1786. Sometimes given as 'Calveley'.
CALVELY John	Of Bruern Stapleford, CHESHIRE Active: 1799-death 1819 Awards: Denbighshire 2 (51009, 51020) (umpire 1: 51006), Flint 5 (52001, 52005, 52010, 52014, 52020) (surveyor 1: 52022) Notes: Calvely died without completing any of his Flint awards as commissioner. Sometimes given as 'Calveley'.
CARTWRIGHT Samuel	Address not given Active 1852-1861 Awards: Denbighshire (surveyor 1: 51005)

CASTREE Josiah	Of Gloucester Land Surveyor Active: 1852-1867 Awards: Radnorshire 1 (58023), ENGLAND 11 Notes: Presumably father of Josiah Castree junior, from whom he cannot always be distinguished.
CHALONER George William	Of Holt Land Surveyor Active: 1817-1848 Awards: Denbighshire 1 (51008)
CHAPMAN Thomas	Of Richmond, SURREY (to 1820); of Middle Temple, LONDON (1821-1836); of Arundel Street, LONDON (1837). Probably lived in Richmond throughout, but with London business addresses. Active: 1805-1837 Awards: Merionethshire 1 (54007), ENGLAND 19
CHEESE John	Of Lyonshall, HEREFORDSHIRE Active: 1806-1824 Awards: Breconshire 1 (47002), Cardiganshire 2 (49004, 49014), Radnorshire 7 (58005, 58008, 58010, 58012, 58022, 58026, 58029), ENGLAND 4 Notes: Possible confusion with son of same name, who was active from 1811 on.
COLLEY Thomas	Of Cefngwifid (Cefngwifed) Active: 1796-death 1812 Awards: Montgomeryshire 1 (56001) (arbitrator 1: 56017)
COULING William	Of Carmarthen (1809-1812); of Brecon (Aberhonddu) (1813) Active: 1809-1813 Awards: Breconshire 1 (47008), Pembrokeshire (surveyor 1: 57004).
DAVID Edward	Of Radyr Court, GLAMORGAN Land Surveyor Active: 1868-1872 Awards: Carmarthenshire 1 (50007), Glamorgan 1 (53001)
DAVID Evan Williams	Of Radyr Court Land Surveyor Active: 1857-1861 Awards: Glamorgan 2 (53005, 53012)

DAVIES Arthur	Of The Hayes, Oswestry, SHROPSHIRE Land Surveyor Active: 1795-death c.1822 Awards: Carmarthenshire 1 (50020), Flint 1 (52004), Montgomeryshire (surveyor 1: 56005), ENGLAND 3
DAVIES David	Of Froodvale (Ffrwd-fâl) in Conwil Cayo (Cynwyl Gaeo), CARMARTHENSHIRE Land Surveyor Active: 1848-1862 Awards: Cardiganshire 5 (49002, 49003, 49007, 49010, 49013), Carmarthenshire 3 (50008, 50011, 50024), Montgomeryshire 3 (56013, 56014, 56016)
DAVIES David	Of Llangatwg (Llangattock) near Crickhowell (Crucywel), BRECONSHIRE Active: 1808-1817 Awards: Breconshire 1 (47012) (surveyor 1: 47002), Monmouthshire 1 (55002) (surveyor 1: 55012), ENGLAND (surveyor 1)
DAVIES Isaac	Of Brecon (Aberhonddu) Land Surveyor Active: 1855-1865 Awards: Breconshire 16 (47001, 47003, 47004, 47006, 47007, 47009, 47010, 47011, 47013, 47014, 47015, 47016, 47017, 47018, 47019, 47020)
DAVIES John	Of Pennal Land Surveyor Active: 1805-1818 Awards: Merionethshire (surveyor 2: 54007, 54008)
DAVIES John Morgan	Of Froodvale (Ffrwd-fâl), CARMARTHENSHIRE Land Surveyor Active: 1863-1888 Awards: Cardiganshire 1 (49009), Carmarthenshire 1(50005)
DAVIS Thomas junior	Of Horningsham (to 1825); of Warminster (from 1825), both WILTSHIRE. Active: 1806-1856 Awards: Monmouthshire 1 (55005), ENGLAND 24 Notes: Son of Thomas senior, from whom he is not always clearly distinguished.
DE BRUYN Henry	Of Southampton Street, LONDON Land Surveyor Active: 1808-1825 Awards: Breconshire 1 (47002), ENGLAND 2

DEW William	Of Bangor, CAERNARFONSHIRE Active: 1859-1861 Awards: Anglesey 1 (46002)
DYER John	Of Cefngwifed Active: 1812-1818 Awards: Montgomeryshire 2 (56001, 56015)
EARL John	Of Overton in Frodsham, CHESHIRE 'Writing Master' Active: 1766-1796 Awards: Flint 1 (52007), ENGLAND 5
EATON Thomas	Of Laugharne (Llacharn), CARMARTHENSHIRE Active: 1815 Awards: Pembrokeshire 1 (57003)
EDWARDS Edward	Of Bron Erch in Aber-erch Active: 1850-1858 Awards: Caernarfonshire 2 (48003, 48006)
EDWARDS John	Of Dolegwyrddon in Lampeter (Llanbedr Pont Steffan) CARDIGANSHIRE Land Surveyor Active: 1850-1855 Awards: Carmarthenshire 1 (50026)
ELLIS Richard	Of Pwllheli Solicitor Active: 1811-1825 Awards: Caernarfonshire 3 (48002, 48008, 48011)
EVANS John	Of Tregynon Active: 1796-1818 Awards: Montgomeryshire (surveyor 1: 56001)
EVANS Samuel	Of Llanrhystud Active: 1853-1860 Awards: Cardiganshire (surveyor 2: 49010, 49013)
EVANS William	Of Llawhaden (Llanhuadain) Vicar Active: 1786 Awards: Pembrokeshire 1 (57008)
EYTON William	Of Gonsal in Condover, SHROPSHIRE Land Agent Active: 1837-1859 Awards: Radnorshire 5 (58001, 58003, 58015, 58016, 58017), ENGLAND 7

FARMER George	Of Montgomery (Trefaldwyn) Land Surveyor Active: 1847-1874 Awards: Flint 1 (52016), ENGLAND 2
FLETCHER Matthew	Of Clifton near Manchester, LANCASHIRE Esquire Active: 1791-1805 Awards: Flint 1 (52009), ENGLAND 1
FOULKES Abraham	Of New Bridge in Ruabon, DENBIGHSHIRE Land Surveyor Active: 1862-1869 Awards: Anglesey 1 (46004), Denbighshire 2 (51012, 51017), Merionethshire 1 (54001)
FRANCIS John	Of Carmarthen (Caerfyrddin) Land Surveyor Active: 1885-1892 Awards: Carmarthenshire 1 (50023)
FULLJAMES Thomas	Of Orpington, KENT (to 1795); of Hasfield Court, GLOUCESTERSHIRE (from 1795) Active: 1789-1843 (died 1847) Awards: Monmouthshire 2 (55004, 55012), ENGLAND 41
GEORGE Richard	Of Montgomery (Trefaldwyn) Active: 1796-c.1805 Awards: Montgomeryshire (surveyor 1: 56001)
GOODE Henry Phelps	Of Haverfordwest (Hwlffordd), PEMBROKESHIRE Land Surveyor Active: 1832-1864 Awards: Carmarthenshire 1 (50027), Pembrokeshire 1 (57002) (surveyor 2: 57006, 57009) Notes: Slater (1851) records as auctioneer and surveyor. Eden lists as active from 1820, and as agent to Lord Milford. Often listed as 'Harry'.
GOODE James	Of Haverfordwest (Hwlffordd) Active: 1815 Awards: Pembrokeshire (surveyor 1: 57003)
GOODE William	Of St Clears (Sanclêr), CARMARTHENSHIRE Land Surveyor Active: 1851-death c.1860 Awards: Carmarthenshire 1 (50002), Pembrokeshire 1 (57005)

GRIFFITH Richard	Of Bangor Clergyman Active: 1788 Awards: Anglesey 1 (46005)
GRIFFITHES Richard	Of Bishops Castle, SHROPSHIRE Active: 1806-1822 Awards: Cardiganshire 1 (49012), Merionethshire 1 (54008), ENGLAND 2
GRIFFITHES Thomas Jones	Of Bishops Castle, SHROPSHIRE Land Agent Active: c.1840-1860 Awards: Cardiganshire 1 (49012), Montgomeryshire 1 (56007), ENGLAND 1 Notes: Sometimes given as 'Griffiths'.
GRIFFITHS Griffith	Of Dolgellau Active: 1805-1809 Awards: Merionethshire 1 (54007)
GRIFFITHS Stephen	Of Llangolmen Esquire Active: 1786 Awards: Pembrokeshire 1 (57008)
HALE Thomas	Of Copthorn, SHROPSHIRE Active: 1780 Awards: Montgomeryshire 1 (56004), ENGLAND (surveyor 1)
HALL Robert Wright	Of Cirencester; later of Gloucester Active: 1801-death 1815 Awards: Monmouthshire (surveyor 1: 55004), ENGLAND 11 (surveyor at least 17)
HAND John	Of Stackpool Court PEMBROKESHIRE (to 1815); of Llangunnor (Llangynnwr) CARMARTHENSHIRE (from 1815). Active: 1788-1820 Awards: Carmarthenshire 1 (50009), Pembrokeshire 2 (57001, 57007) (surveyor 1: 57003)
HAND William	Of Llangunnor (Llangynnwr) CARMARTHENSHIRE (to 1820); of Molleston, PEMBROKESHIRE (from 1820). Land Agent Active: 1815-1854 Awards: Carmarthenshire 2 (50008, 50009)

HARRIS
Samuel Joseph
Of Hereford
Active: 1813-1815
Awards: Monmouthshire (surveyor 1: 55002), ENGLAND 2 (surveyor 1)

HARVEY
John
Of Haverfordwest (Hwlffordd)
Land Agent
Active: 1832-1833
Awards: Pembrokeshire 1 (57006)

HARVEY
Robert
Of Dunstal in Abbots Bromley, STAFFORDSHIRE
Active: 1800-death 1835
Awards: Denbighshire 2 (51013, 51023) (assistant commissioner 1: 51018), ENGLAND 19

HASSALL
Charles
Of Eastwood in Narberth (Arbeth), PEMBROKESHIRE
Land Surveyor
Born 1754 (Eden). Active: 1786-death 1814.
Awards: Cardiganshire 2 (49012, 49014), Carmarthenshire 8 (50009, 50010, 50013, 50014, 50018, 50021, 50022, 50028), Merionethshire 2 (54007, 54008), Pembrokeshire 1 (57004) (surveyor 1: 57008).

HASSALL
Thomas
Of Kilrhue (Cilrhiw near Narberth), PEMBROKESHIRE
Active: 1809-death 1813
Awards: Cardiganshire 1 (49012), Carmarthenshire 4 (50009, 50010, 50015, 50020), Pembrokeshire 1 (57004)
Notes: Brother of Charles.

HEYS
James
Of Knowsley, LANCASHIRE
Active: 1791-1816
Awards: Flint (surveyor 1: 52009), ENGLAND 5

HILL
Richard
Of Farley, SHROPSHIRE (1771-1792); of Stellington, STAFFORDSHIRE (from 1793).
Active: 1791-death c.1795
Awards: Flint 2 (52002, 52009), ENGLAND 14

HOLLIER
Henry
Of Cardiff (Caerdydd)
Active: 1801-1809
Awards: Glamorgan 1 (53002)

HOPKIN(S)
William
Of Troserchfawr in Llangennech, CARMARTHENSHIRE
Active: 1807-1816
Awards: Carmarthenshire 3 (50014, 50022, 50028)

HORNE W. B.	Address not given Active: 1936 Awards: Glamorgan 1 (53003)
HOWELL John	Of Penyrheol Esquire Active: 1807 Awards: Carmarthenshire 1 (50028)
HUGHES Edward Jones	Of Mold (Yr Wyddgrug) 1809; of Plas Onn (1819), both FLINT (1819). Active: 1811–death 1835 Awards: Denbighshire 2 (51009, 51018) (surveyor 1: 51011), Flint 1 (52005)
HUGHES Hugh	Of Aberystwyth Active: 1815 Awards: Cardiganshire 1 (49004)
HUGHES John	Of Aberystwyth Active: 1812–1816 Awards: Cardiganshire (surveyor 2: 49004, 49014)
HUGHES John	Address not given Land Surveyor Active: 1852–1861 Awards: Denbighshire (surveyor 1: 51005)
HUMPHREYS John	Of Tyn-y-coed in Berriew (Aberriw), MONTGOMERYSHIRE. Active: c.1800–1828 Awards: Montgomeryshire 1 (56015) (surveyor 1: 56001) Notes: Possibly the Humphreys recorded by Dodd in Flint (52020)
HUMPHREYS William	Of Berriew (Aberriw) Active: 1816–1826 Awards: Montgomeryshire (surveyor 1: 56015) Notes: Son of John (see Jones, 1985).
IVESON John	Of Halliford, MIDDLESEX Active: 1840–1843 Awards: Radnorshire 1 (58023), ENGLAND 2
JEBB Richard	Of Oswestry, SHROPSHIRE (to 1809); of Chirk, (Y Waun) DENBIGHSHIRE (from 1810). Active: 1809–1824 Awards: Denbighshire 1 (51011) (surveyor 1: 51004), Merionethshire 1 (54003)

JENKINS David Joel	Of Lampeter (Llanbedr Pont Steffan) Active: 1812-1816 Awards: Cardiganshire 3 (49004, 49012, 49014)
JONES David	Of Llanfyllin Active: 1828 Awards: Montgomeryshire 1 (56009)
JONES Edward	Of Plas Ucha in Whitford (Chwitffordd) Active: 1811-1828 Awards: Flint (surveyor 1: 52014)
JONES John	Of Plas Isaf (Issa) in Llangar, MERIONETHSHIRE Active: 1814-1836 Awards: Denbighshire (assistant commissioner 1: 51018) Notes: Possibly same as the assistant commissioner at Caernarfon (48004). Given as 'of Corwen'.
JONES Richard	Of Pantirrion (Panthirion) near St Dogmaels (Llandudoch) CARDIGANSHIRE Land Surveyor Active: 1808-death 1818 Awards: Cardiganshire 1 (49012), Carmarthenshire 2 (50009, 50021), Pembrokeshire 1 (57004)
JONES Robert	Of Ruthin (Rhuthun), DENBIGHSHIRE Active: 1802-c.1810 Awards: Denbighshire 1 (51023)
JONES Thomas	Of Denbigh (Dinbych) Land Surveyor Active: 1850-death 1864 Awards: Anglesey 1 (46004), Denbighshire 1 (51022), Flint 1 (52011)
JONES Thomas	Of Lymore Hall (to c.1800); of Penbryn, (from c.1800). Active: 1796-1803 Awards: Montgomeryshire 1 (56001)
JONES Thomas junior	Of Penbryn, MONTGOMERYSHIRE Active: 1821-1845 Awards: Cardiganshire 1 (49012), Montgomeryshire 1 (56006)
JONES Walter	Of Cefn Rug in Corwen, MERIONETHSHIRE Active: 1806-death 1815 Awards: Anglesey 1 (46003), Caernarfonshire 5 (48007, 48008, 48009, 48010, 48013),

	Denbighshire 4 (51006, 51009, 51018, 51020), Merionethshire 2 (54004, 54005) (assistant commissioner 1: 54002)
JONES William	Of Llanidloes Active: 1816-1826 Awards: Montgomeryshire (surveyor 1: 56015)
KYFFIN Thomas	Of Copthorn, SHROPSHIRE Active: 1788-1826 Awards: Montgomeryshire 1 (56012) (surveyor 4: 56005, 56008, 56011, 56018), ENGLAND (surveyor 5)
LEWIS John	Of Kincoed (Cyncoed) (to c.1860); of Gwarallt (from c.1860), both in Llandefeilog (Llandyfaelog) Active: 1852-1868 Awards: Carmarthenshire 5 (50003, 50004, 50016, 50017, 50025)
LINTON James	Of Loveston Active: 1788 Awards: Pembrokeshire 1 (57001)
LLOYD Evan	Of Maesyporth Active: 1788 Awards: Anglesey 1 (46005)
LLOYD Jonathan	Of Trefcoed Esquire Active: 1761 Awards: Montgomeryshire 1 (56019)
LLOYD Thomas	Of Trefnant Esquire Active: 1761 Awards: Montgomeryshire 1 (56019)
LLOYD Thomas	Of Denbigh (Dinbych) Active: 1800-1805 Awards: Denbighshire 1 (51013)
LOVETT Thomas	Of Chirk (Y Waun), DENBIGHSHIRE Active: 1789-1805 Awards: Denbighshire 1 (51013), Montgomeryshire (arbitrator 1: 56009)
MARSTON Francis	Of Hopesay, SHROPSHIRE Esquire Active: 1840-1843 Awards: Denbighshire 1 (51014)

MATTHEWS John	Of Newmarket (Trelawnyd), FLINT (to 1805); of Plasynllysfaen (Plas yn Llysfaen), CAERNARFONSHIRE (from 1805) Active: 1792-death 1830 Awards: Denbighshire 3 (51001, 51007, 51020), Flint 6 (52002, 52013, 52017, 52018, 52019, 52022)
MATTHEWS John	Of Pen-y-bont in Mold (Y Wyddgrug), FLINT (to 1823); of Clydfane near Llanidloes, MONTGOMERYSHIRE (1823-1828); of Aberystwyth, CARDIGANSHIRE (from 1828). Born 1733, died 1848. Active: 1807-1831 Awards: Caernarfonshire 1 (48012), Denbighshire 3 (51002, 51006, 51020), Flint 1 (52014), Montgomeryshire 1 (56015)
MATTHEWS Thomas	Of Shelderton, SHROPSHIRE Active: 1772-1803 Awards: Montgomeryshire 4 (56001, 56004, 56005, 56010) (arbitrator 1: 56009), ENGLAND 5
MAUGHAN John	Of Hitchen, HERTFORDSHIRE (to 1810); of Luton, BEDFORDSHIRE (1810- c.1820); of Oswestry, SHROPSHIRE (1821-c.1830); of Barnt Green, WORCESTERSHIRE (from 1831). Active: 1797-1843 Awards: Anglesey 2 (46006, 46007), Denbighshire 4 (51002, 51006, 51010, 51020), Flint 1 (52021), Montgomeryshire 1 (56015), ENGLAND 11
MICKLEBURGH Charles	Of Montgomery (Trefaldwyn) Active: 1837-death c.1862 Awards: Cardiganshire (surveyor 1: 49012), Denbighshire 2 (51016, 51021), Montgomeryshire 1 (56003) (surveyor 2: 56006, 56011), Radnorshire 2 (58033, 58034) (surveyor 1: 58016, umpire 1: 58023), ENGLAND 2
MICKLEBURGH John	Of Montgomery (Trefaldwyn) Land Surveyor Active: 1852-1891 Awards: Radnorshire 4 (58014, 58020, 58021, 58027), ENGLAND 5
MORGAN Thomas	Of Cardiff (Caerdydd) Active: 1801-1809 Awards: Glamorgan 1 (53002)

MORGAN William	Of Llandingal Land Surveyor Active: 1859-1867 Awards: Carmarthenshire 1 (50006)
MORLEY Thomas	Of St Michael Cwmdu (Llanfihangel Cwm Du) Active: 1814-1817 Awards: Breconshire 1 (47012)
MORRIS George	Of Plasissa in Llangennech Land Surveyor Active: 1808-1818 Awards: Carmarthenshire 3 (50012, 50013, 50021)
MYTTON Devereux	Of Guilsfield (Cegidfa) Esquire Active: 1761 Awards: Montgomeryshire 1 (56019)
NUTTALL George	Of Hampton Court Park, and of Leominster, HEREFORDSHIRE Active: 1814-death 1820 Awards: Montgomeryshire 1 (56015), ENGLAND 3 Notes: Agent to Sir Richard Arkwright
OWEN George	Of Oswestry, SHROPSHIRE Land Surveyor Active: 1860-1869 Awards: Radnorshire 2 (58006, 58018)
PARRY Edward Powell	Of Morfodion, Llanidloes Land Surveyor Active: 1852-1865 Awards: Montgomeryshire 1 (56016), ENGLAND 1
PARRY William	Of Morfodion, Llanidloes Active: 1852-death c.1855 Awards: Montgomeryshire 1 (56016), ENGLAND 1
PAYNTER David	Of Pembroke Attorney at Law Active: 1788 Awards: Pembrokeshire 1 (57001)
PETERS Robert	Of Mold (Y Wyddgrug), FLINT Active: 1814-1836 Awards: Denbighshire 1 (51018)

PHELPS George	Of Studda Active: 1786 Awards: Pembrokeshire 1 (57008)
PHILPOTT Henry	Of Haverfordwest (Hwlffordd) Active: 1863-1869 Awards: Pembrokeshire (surveyor 2: 57009, 57010)
PIERCY Richard	Address not given Active: 1843-1849 Awards: Caernarfonshire (surveyor 1: 48004)
PIERCY Robert A.	Of Llanidloes Active: 1816-1826 Awards: Montgomeryshire (surveyor 1: 56015)
PIERCY Robert	Of Mold (Y Wyddgrug) Active: 1800-1805 Awards: Flint (surveyor 1: 52018)
PLESCINS Thomas Bridgen	Of Welshpool (Y Trallwng); later of Crackley Bank, SHROPSHIRE Yeoman, later Surveyor Active: 1788-1801 Awards: Montgomeryshire (surveyor 1: 56005)
POTTS Josiah	Of Ollerton, CHESHIRE Active: 1791-1807 Awards: Denbighshire (assistant commissioner 3: 51006, 51009, 51020), Flint 3 (52002, 52008, 52013) (assistant commissioner 3: 52010, 52014, 52018), ENGLAND 7
POUNDLEY John Wilkes	Of Kerry (Ceri), MONTGOMERYSHIRE Land Surveyor Active: 1853-1863 Awards: Denbighshire 2 (51003, 51005)
PRICE Henry	Of Hereford Active: 1811-1812 Awards: Monmouthshire 1 (55002), ENGLAND 1.
PRICE Richard	Of Knighton (Trefyclo), RADNORSHIRE Active: 1779-1784 Awards: Montgomeryshire 1 (56004), ENGLAND 2
PUGH William	Of Trefllan Active: 1797-1804 Awards: Montgomeryshire (surveyor 1: 56001)

PUGH William	Of Caer Howell Barrister Active: 1816 Awards: Montgomeryshire 1 (56015; in fact took no part)
RAWLINSON J. S.	Address not given Active: 1866-1870 Awards: Anglesey (assistant commissioner 1: 46002)
REES John	Of Cilgellissa in Pencarreg Land Surveyor Active: 1854-1858 Awards: Cardiganshire 1 (49006)
REES John William	Of Pencarreg in Llanilar Active: 1850-1864 Awards: Cardiganshire 2 (49001, 49015)
ROBERTS Edward Griffith	Of Caernarfon Active: 1812-1825 Awards: Anglesey (assistant commissioner 1: 46006), Caernarfonshire (assistant commissioner 1: 48008)
ROBERTS John	Of Ruthin (Rhuthun) Active: 1802-1820 Awards: Denbighshire 1 (51023)
ROBERTS Richard	Of Rose Hill, St Asaph (Llanelwy) Active: 1863-1871 Awards: Denbighshire 1 (51022)
ROBERTS Thomas	Of Brynselwrn, MERIONETHSHIRE Active: 1806-1830 Awards: Caernarfonshire 3 (48009, 48010, 48013) (surveyor 1: 48007)
ROBERTS Thomas	Of The Wern, SHROPSHIRE Active: 1810-1825 Awards: Merionethshire (surveyor 1: 54003)
ROBINSON Charles Barnes	Of Hill Ridware, STAFFORDSHIRE Active: 1802-death 1810 Awards: Denbighshire 1 (51023)
ROCH Nicholas	Of Paskeston Esquire Active: 1786 Awards: Pembrokeshire 1 (57008)

ROE Frederick Adair	Address not given Active: 1816 Awards: Montgomeryshire 1 (56015; in fact took no part)
ROGERS Edward	Of Manachlog; later of Bryn Eithin, both in Northop, FLINT Active: 1809-1850 Awards: Denbighshire (surveyor 1: 51009), Flint 2 (52001, 52010)
ROYLE James	Of Caermelwr, DENBIGHSHIRE Active: 1806-death 1826 Awards: Merionethshire 1 (54005)
SAUNDERS Thomas	Of Lampeter (Llanbedr Pont Steffan), CARDIGANSHIRE Active: 1848-1854 Awards: Breconshire 1 (47005), Carmarthenshire 1 (50019)
SAYCE Edward Morris	Of Kington, HEREFORDSHIRE Land Surveyor Active: 1847-1851 Awards: Radnorshire 2 (58009, 58011)
SAYCE Maurice (Morris)	Of Kington, HEREFORDSHIRE Active: 1811-1829 Awards: Radnorshire 1 (58030) (surveyor 1: 58029)
SAYCE William	Of Kington, HEREFORDSHIRE Land Surveyor Active: 1828-1829 Awards: Radnorshire (surveyor 1: 58030)
SIMON John	Of Ruthin (Rhuthun) Active: 1809-1836 Awards: Denbighshire (surveyor 2: 51011, 51018)
SMITH George	Of Northampton Land Surveyor Active: 1869-1877 Awards: Denbighshire 1 (51019)
SMITH Richard	Of Cheadle, STAFFORDSHIRE Active: 1791-1831 Awards: Flint (surveyor 1: 52009), ENGLAND 3.
SMITH Robert	Of Carmarthen (Caerfyrddin) Active: 1814-1819 Awards: Carmarthenshire 1 (50001)

STELFOX Edward	Of Sunderland in Bowden, CHESHIRE Active: 1778-1781 Awards: Flint 1 (52007)
STEPHENS James	Of Presteigne (Llanandras) Active: 1810-1820 Awards: Radnorshire 7 (58005, 58008, 58010, 58012, 58022, 58026, 58029), ENGLAND 1
TAMLYN John	Of Mount Pleasant, Haverfordwest (Hwlffordd) Active: 1815 Awards: Pembrokeshire (surveyor 1: 57003)
TAMLYN Thomas	Of Castle Terrace, Haverfordwest (Hwlffordd) Active: 1863-1869 Awards: Pembrokeshire 1 (57010)
TENCH John	Of Ludlow, SHROPSHIRE Active: 1848-1867 Awards: Radnorshire 1 (58028), ENGLAND 3
THOMAS Daniel	Of Frondeg in Llanbadarn Fawr Active: 1862-1872 Awards: Cardiganshire 2 (49008, 49011)
THOMAS George	Of Brechfa Land Surveyor Active: 1811 Awards: Carmarthenshire 1 (50018)
THOMAS Griffith	Of Maentwrog, MERIONETHSHIRE Active: 1808-death 1813 Awards: Caernarfonshire (assistant commissioner 1: 48008)
THOMAS John	Of Trevallyn, DENBIGHSHIRE Active: 1791-death c.1792 Awards: Flint 1 (52009), ENGLAND 1
VERNON Thomas	Of Oswestry, SHROPSHIRE Active: 1772-1789 Awards: Flint 1 (52006), ENGLAND 4
VICKERS Valentine senior	Of Cranmere, SHROPSHIRE Born c.1746 (Eden). Active: 1795-death 1815 Awards: Montgomeryshire 2 (56011, 56012), ENGLAND 6

VICKERS Valentine junior	Of Cranmere, SHROPSHIRE Active: 1793-1830 Awards: Montgomeryshire 5 (56001, 56008, 56011, 56017, 56018), ENGLAND 11 Notes: Son of Valentine senior, worked with him, and took over several enclosures on his father's death.
WATERS John	Of Treventy Esquire Active: 1807 Awards: Carmarthenshire 1 (50028)
WATTS John	Of Sulgrave, NORTHAMPTONSHIRE Active: 1762-1787 Awards: Monmouthshire 1 (55003), ENGLAND 64 Notes: Watts was also highly active as quality man and surveyor in England.
WEDGE John	Of Goodig in Pembrey (Pen-bre) Active: 1813-1843 Awards: Carmarthenshire 1 (50015) Notes: Possibly a relative of the other Wedges who were active as commissioners in the West Midlands and East Anglia.
WEDGE Thomas	Of Sealand, CHESHIRE Active: 1794-c.1815 Awards: Flint 3 (52008, 52010, 52019) Notes: Eden records as engineer. His role in 52019 is not clear.
WESTON Robert	Of Brackley, (to 1799); of Aynho (from 1779), both NORTHAMPTONSHIRE Active: 1762-1808 Awards: Monmouthshire 1 (55003), ENGLAND 37 Notes: Also very active in England as a surveyor.
WESTON Samuel	Of Chester (1780); of Halewood, LANCASHIRE (1790) Active: 1791-1797 Awards: Flint 1 (52009)
WHARTON Samuel	Of Gray's Inn, LONDON Active: 1808-1817 Awards: Breconshire (surveyor 1: 47002), ENGLAND 1
WHILTON Thomas	Of Tyrley, STAFFORDSHIRE Active: 1775-1801 Awards: Flint 1 (52006), ENGLAND 1

WILLIAMS Edward	Of Garreglloyd near Mold (Y Wyddgrug) Active: 1811-1846 Awards: Flint (assistant commissioner 1: 52010)
WILLIAMS James Peachey	Of St Werburgh, Bristol Land Surveyor Active: 1853-1870 Awards: Glamorgan 3 (53006, 53009, 53011), Monmouthshire 7 (55001, 55006, 55007, 55008, 55009, 55010, 55013), ENGLAND 3 Notes: Eden records 'of Beachley 1828'. Possibly another of same name.
WILLIAMS John	Of Treffos Vicar Active: 1788-1821 Awards: Anglesey 1 (46005)
WILLIAMS John junior	Of Tregarnedd Active: 1811-1821 Awards: Anglesey 1 (46005)
WILLIAMS Richard Bowen	Of Horeb in Pembrey (Pen-bre) Active: 1814-1819 Awards: Carmarthenshire (surveyor 2: 50001, 50015)
WILLIAMS Robert	Of Ty Coch, Llandegai (Llandygai), CAERNARFONSHIRE Active: 1806-1836 Awards: Caernarfonshire 1 48011), Cardiganshire 1 (49012), Merionethshire 1 (54006) (surveyor 2: 54004, 54005)
WILLIAMS Stephen William	Of Rhayader (Rhaeadr Gwy) Land Surveyor Active: 1862-1885 Awards: Radnorshire 8 (58002, 58007, 58013, 58019, 58024, 58025, 58031, 58032), ENGLAND 1
WILLIAMS Thomas	Of Henllan Active: 1802-1814 Awards: Denbighshire (surveyor 1: 51007)
WILLIAMS William	Of Carreg Llwydd near Mold (Y Wyddgrug), FLINT Active: 1808-1831 Awards: Denbighshire (assistant commissioner 5: 51001, 51002, 51006, 51009, 51020) Flint 1 (52015) (surveyor 1: 52021, assistant commissioner 2: 52010, 52014)

WILLIAMS William	Of Tir isha, St Brides Minor (Llansanffraid-ar-Ogwr) Land Surveyor Active: 1868-1871 Awards: Glamorgan 1 (53004)
WILLIAMS William	Of Dolgelley (Dolgellau) Active: 1814-1827 Awards: Merionethshire 1 (54005)
WILSON John	Address not given Barrister Active: 1838-1840 Awards: Pembrokeshire 1 (57009)
WILSON Lewis	Of Langdon in Begelly (Begeli) Land Surveyor Active: 1856-1868 Awards: Pembrokeshire 1 (57005)
WYATT Benjamin	Of Lime Grove (1802); of The Terrace (1814), both CAERNARFONSHIRE Architect Born 1744 (Eden). Active: 1802-death 1818 Awards: Anglesey 1 (46005), Caernarfonshire 1 (48001)
WYATT James	Of Lime Grove, CAERNARFONSHIRE Born 1795, died 1862 (Eden). Active: 1818-1821 Awards: Anglesey 1 (46005)
WYATT Samuel	Of Seany (Sinai) Park near Burton (to 1774); of Burton (from 1774), both STAFFORDSHIRE Born 1736. Active: 1760-death 1807 Awards: Flint 2 (52007, 52013), ENGLAND 87 Notes: One of the principal English commissioners, and son of William Wyatt, himself a major commissioner.
WYLEY William	Of Admaston, SHROPSHIRE Active: 1806-1835 Awards: Montgomeryshire 2 (56002, 56018), ENGLAND 4
WYNN Henry	Of Doleardden Esquire Active: 1761 Awards: Montgomeryshire 1 (56019; in fact took no part)

YATES
Richard

Of Whittington, SHROPSHIRE(to c.1843); of Gravel Hill, MONTGOMERYSHIRE (c.1843-1852); of Oswestry (from 1852).
Active: 1815-death c.1860
Awards: Anglesey 1 (46007) (surveyor 1: 46003), Caernarfonshire 1 (48004), Denbighshire 2 (51005, 51021) (surveyor 1: 51016).

BIBLIOGRAPHY

BOWEN, I. (1914) *The Great Enclosures of Common Lands in Wales* (Chiswick).

CHAPMAN, J. (1972) 'Agriculture and the "Waste" in Monmouthshire from 1750 to the Present Day' (Unpublished PhD thesis, University of London).

CHAPMAN, J. (1978) 'Some Problems in the Interpretation of Enclosure Awards', *Agricultural History Review*, 26, 108-114.

CHAPMAN, J. (1987) 'The Extent and Nature of Parliamentary Enclosure', *Agricultural History Review*, 35, 25-35.

CHAPMAN, J. (1991) 'The Later Parliamentary Enclosures of South Wales', *Agricultural History Review*, 39 (in press).

CLARK, A. (1972) 'Enclosures in Monmouthshire', *Severn and Wye Review*, 2, 1.

COLYER, R.J. (1977) 'The Enclosure and Drainage of Cors Fochno, 1813-47', *Ceredigion*, 2, 181-192.

DAVIES, A.E. (1976) 'Enclosures in Cardiganshire, 1750-1850', *Ceredigion*, 8, 100-140.

DAVIES, M. (1955-6) 'Common Lands in South East Monmouthshire', *Transactions of the Cardiff Naturalists Society*, 85.

DAVIES, W. (1813) *A General View of the Agriculture of North Wales* (London). (Commonly known as the 'Board of Agriculture Report'.)

DAVIES, W. (1815) *A General View of the Agriculture of South Wales* (London), 2 vols. (Commonly known as the 'Board of Agriculture Report'.)

DAVIES, W.L. (1937-9) 'The Enclosure Award of Henllan Common Lands and Denbigh Green', *Bulletin of the Board of Celtic Studies*, 9, 247-271.

DODD, A.H. (1927) 'The Enclosure Movement in North Wales', *Bulletin of the Board of Celtic Studies*, 3, 216-238.

EDWARDS, J.W. (1963) 'Enclosure and agricultural improvement in the Vale of Clwyd, 1750-1875' (Unpublished MA thesis, University of London).

EVANS, D.G. (1983-4) 'The Hope Enclosure Act of 1791', *Flintshire Historical Society Journal*, 31, 161-186.

HASSALL, C. (1812) *A General View of the Agriculture of the County of Monmouth* (London).

JEFFREYS JONES, J.T. (1959) *Acts of Parliament concerning Wales, 1714-1901* (Cardiff).

JONES, E.J. (1924) 'The Enclosure Movement in Anglesey, 1784-1866' (Unpublished MA thesis, University of Wales).

JONES, E.J. (1925-6) 'The Enclosure Movement in Anglesey, 1784-1866', *Transactions of the Anglesey Antiquarian and Field Club*, 21-58, 1925, and 51-89, 1926.

JONES, G.R.J. (1964) 'The Llanynys quillets: a measure of landscape transformation', *Transaction of the Denbighshire Historical Society*, 13, 133-158.

JONES, I.E. (1972) 'The Township of Llysgyn, Carno', *Montgomery Collections*, 62, 202-211.
JONES, I.E. (1983) 'The Arwystli Enclosures, 1816-1828', *Montgomery Collections*, 71, 61-69.
JONES, I.E. (1985) 'The Enclosure of the Llanidloes and Caersws Commons', *Montgomery Collections*, 73, 54-68.
JONES, I.E. (1985) 'The Arwystli (Montgomeryshire) Enclosures, 1816-1828', University of Birmingham Occasional Publication, 18.
JONES, J.G. (1981) 'The Wynn Estate of Gwidir: Aspects of its Growth and Development, c1500-1850', *National Library of Wales Journal*, 22, 2.
JONES, M.C. (1879) 'The Enclosure of Common Lands in Montgomeryshire', *Montgomery Collections*, 12, 267-88.
LEWIS, W.J. (1962) 'A Disturbance on Llanrhystud Mountain', *Ceredigion*, 4, 312-313.
LLOYD, J. (1905) *The Great Forest of Brecknock* (London).
MORGAN, C. (1959) 'The Effect of Parliamentary enclosure on the landscape of Caernarvonshire and Merioneth' (Unpublished MSc thesis, University of Wales).
PARLIAMENTARY PAPERS (1843) 'Return of the Tithe Commission of Common Land in Wales', 325.
PARLIAMENTARY PAPERS (1904) 'Return of all Inclosure Awards or Copies.... at the present time deposited or enrolled with the Clerkes of the Peace', 50.
PARLIAMENTARY PAPERS (1914) 'Inclosure acts: return in chronological order of all acts passed for the inclosure of commons or waste lands, separately, in England and Wales', 399.
PLUME, G.A. (1935) 'The Enclosure Movement in Caernarvonshire, with special reference to the Porth-yr-Aur Papers' (Unpublished MA thesis, University of Wales).
POWELL, J.M. (1962) 'An Economic Geography of Montgomeryshire in the Nineteenth Century' (Unpublished MA thesis, University of Liverpool).
POWELL, J.M. (1967-8) 'Agriculture in Montgomeryshire in the early nineteenth century', *Montgomery Collections*, 60, 67-84.
PRYCE, W.T.R. (1961-2) 'Enclosure and field patterns in the Banwy valley', *Montgomery Collections*, 57, 23-32.
REES, W. (1966) *The Great Forest of Brecknock* (Brecon).
ROYAL COMMISION (1896) 'Report of the Royal Commission on Land in Wales and Monmouthshire', 1893-1896.
SHAW LEFEVRE, G. (1894) *English commons and forests: the story of the battle during the last 30 years over the commons and forests of England and Wales* (London).
SINCLAIR, SIR J. (1802) 'Report from the Select Committee on the Cultivation and Improvement of the Wastes, Uninclosed and Unproductive Lands of the Kingdom', *Reports from the Committees of the House of Commons*, 10 (1774-1802).
SYLVESTER, D. (1969) *The Rural Landscape of the Welsh Borderland* (London).

THOMAS, C. (1965) 'The Evolution of Rural Settlement and Land Tenure in Merioneth' (Unpublished PhD thesis, University of Wales).
THOMAS, C. (1971) 'The Corsygedol Estate during "The Age of Improvement"', *Journal of the Merioneth Historical and Record Society*, 303-310.
THOMAS, C. (1975) 'Colonization, Enclosure and the Rural Landscape', *National Library of Wales Journal*, 19, 133-146.
THOMAS, C. (1985) 'Land Surveyors in Wales, 1750-1850: the Matthews Family', *Bulletin of the Board of Celtic Studies*, 32, 216-232.
THOMAS, J.G. (1957) 'Some Enclosure Patterns in Central Wales: a study in landscape modification', *Geography*, 42, 25-36.
THOMAS, J.G. (1955) 'The Distribution of the Commons in Part of Arwystli at the Time of Enclosure', *Montgomery Collections*, 54, 27-33.
WILLIAMS, D. (1952) 'Rhyfel y Sais Bach. An Enclosure Riot on Mynydd Bach', *Ceredigion*, 2, 39-52.
WILLIAMS, M. (1970) 'The Enclosure and Reclamation of Waste Land in England and Wales in the Eighteenth and Nineteenth Centuries', *Trans Institute of British Geographers*, 51, 55-69.
WORTHINGTON, R.A. (1956) 'The Growth of Rural Settlement in South East Monmouthshire' (Unpublished MA thesis, University of Wales).

APPENDIX

In addition to the Parliamentary enclosures affecting Wales, and listed in this guide, and those for England given in Tate's Domesday, a small number of enclosure Acts for Ireland and Scotland was passed by the united Parliament in London. These Acts are listed below for completeness, though no attempt has been made to trace any of the details of the awards. All these enclosures are believed to have consisted of common and waste.

Enclosure Acts for Ireland

a) Dublin

Garristown	1803	1190 acres
Kilmainham, St James, Clondalkin, Crumlin, Newcastle and Rathcoole	1818	Area not given.
Portrane	1803	Area not given
Saggart	1816	900 acres
Tallaght, Lusk and Kilsallaghan	1821	783, 320, and 150 acres respectively

N.B. Andrews also records Rathcoole, 1811. I can find no reference to this in the House of Lords Record Office, nor is there mention of Rathcoole under the Lyons etc. Act below (see Kildare).

b) Kerry

Castle Island	1824	1020 acres.

c) Kildare

Ballymore Eustace	1814	320 acres (listed as County Dublin in act)
Clane and Manheim	1819	426 acres
Lyons, Kill, Clonclis, Celbridge, and Donnacomport.	1811	373 acres.

d) Kilkenny

Gowran	1814	182 acres
Callan, Coolagh, and Knocktopher	1829	1028 acres

e) Limerick

Rathkeale and Croagh	1839	578 acres

f) Tipperary

Mealiffe, Upper Church, and Temple Beg	1834	3500 acres

Enclosure Act for Scotland

Fife

Falkland and Strathmiglo	1815

INDEX OF PLACES ENCLOSED

Abaty Cwm-hir, or Abbeycwmhir (Radnorshire) 58016
Aberdâr, or Aberdare (Glamorgan) 53001
Aberdaron (Caernarfonshire) 48001, 48002
Aber-erch (Caernarfonshire) 48002
Abergele (Denbighshire) 51001
Abergwili, or Abergwilly (Carmarthenshire) 50001, 50002
Aberhafesb (Montgomeryshire) 56001
Aber-nant (Carmarthenshire) 50003, 50004
Aberriw (Montgomeryshire) 56001
Abertawe (Glamorgan) 53010
Aberteifi (Cardiganshire) 49002
Afon Dyfyrdwy (Flint) 52003
Alberbury (Shropshire, formerly partly in Montgomeryshire) 56002
Alexanderstone (Breconshire) 47008
Allt-mawr (Breconshire) 47007
Allt Melyd (Flint) 52012, 52019
Allt yr Onon (Breconshire) 47008
Arrowry, The (Flint) 52006
Arustley, or Arwstlli (Montgomeryshire) 56015
Aston (Montgomeryshire) 56004
Axton (Flint) 52010
Bachau (Montgomeryshire) 56010
Backs Common (Glamorgan) 53009
Banhadla Ucha (Denbighshire) 51021
Bannel (Flint) 52008
Barelands (Monmouthshire) 55008
Barmouth Marsh (Merionethshire) 54004
Battle, or Y Batel (Breconshire) 47001
Bausley (Montgomeryshire) 56002
Beguildy (Radnorshire) 58001, 58014
Ben Acre (Monmouthshire) 55009
Bermoss Green (Flint) 52006
Berriew, or Berriw (Montgomeryshire) 56001
Berwick Hamlet (Carmarthenshire) 50014
Bettisfield Moss (Flint) 52006
Betws (Montgomeryshire) 56001
Betws Abergele (Denbighshire) 51002
Betws Commons (Merionethshire) 54001
Betws Disserth (Radnorshire) 58002
Betws Gwerful Goch (Denbighshire) 51003
Betws Gwerful Goch (Merionethshire) 54001
Betws Hills (Denbighshire) 51003
Betws-yn-Rhos (Denbighshire) 51002
Bishton (Monmouthshire) 55007, 55011
Blaenmeherin (Cardiganshire) 49005
Blaenpathnog (Montgomeryshire) 56007
Blaenpennal (Cardiganshire) 49001
Bleddfa (Radnorshire) 58003
Bochrwyd (Radnorshire) 58004
Bodafon (Anglesey) 46001
Bodfach (Montgomeryshire) 56012
Bodyddan (Montgomeryshire) 56012

Bodlowydd (Denbighshire) 51011
Boughrood (Radnorshire) 58004
Braden Heath (Flint) 52006
Braichystyn (Caernarfonshire) 48002
Brecknock Forest (Breconshire) 47002
Brecon Manor (Breconshire) 47009, 47010
Brickhill (Flint) 52001
Broadmead (Monmouthshire) 55008
Bronington Green (Flint) 52006
Bronllys (Breconshire) 47003
Broughton (Flint) 52008
Bryn Brion (Denbighshire) 51018
Bryn Cymme (Denbighshire) 51011
Brynelltyn (Montgomeryshire) 56012
Bryn Postig (Montgomeryshire) 56013
Brwynllys (Breconshire) 47003
Bryncroes (Caernarfonshire) 48001, 48002
Bryneglwys (Denbighshire) 51009
Bryngwaeddau (Montgomeryshire) 56008
Bryn Mulan (Denbighshire) 51018
Bugeildy (Radnorshire) 58001, 58014
Burroughs (Glamorgan) 53010
Buttington (Montgomeryshire) 56004
Bwlchcynbyd (Carmarthenshire) 50018
Bwlchderwin (Caernarfonshire) 48011
Bwlch Gwallter (Cardiganshire) 49005
Bwlch Mawr (Caernarfonshire) 48011
Caeo (Carmarthenshire) 50022
Caerdydd (Glamorgan) 53002
Caereinion, Castle (Montgomeryshire) 56011, 56016
Caereinion Iscoed (Montgomeryshire) 56001
Caereinion Uwchcoed (Montgomeryshire) 56008
Caergybi (Anglesey) 46002
Caerhun, or Caerhyn (Caernarfonshire) 48003
Caernarfon, or Caernarvon (Caernarfonshire) 48005
Caerwys (Flint) 52001
Caldicot (Monmouthshire) 55001, 55009
Camddwr (Cardiganshire) 49009
Canton (Glamorgan) 53002
Cantref, or Cantriff (Breconshire) 47015
Cantremellenith (Radnorshire) 58026
Cardiff (Glamorgan) 53002
Cardigan (Cardiganshire) 49002
Carn Fadryn (Caernarfonshire) 48008
Carnfanole (Breconshire) 47016
Carnguwch (Caernarfonshire) 48011
Carno (Montgomeryshire) 56015
Casgob (Radnorshire) 58005
Casllwchwr (Glamorgan) 53007
Casnewydd-ar-Wysg (Monmouthshire) no number
Castell Caereinion (Montgomeryshire) 56011, 56016
Castlemartin, or Castellmartin (Pembrokeshire) 57001
Castlewright (Montgomeryshire) 56004
Cathedine (Breconshire) 47004

Cathiniog (Carmarthenshire) 50020
Cayo (Carmarthenshire) 50022
Cedewain (Montgomeryshire) 56001
Cefn (Montgomeryshire) 56007
Cefn Arthen (Breconshire) 47005
Cefn Collon (Denbighshire) 51013
Cefn Drawen (Radnorshire) 58002, 58013
Cefn Du (Caernarfonshire) 48010
Cefn Erthan (Breconshire) 47005
Cefn Erthan (Carmarthenshire) 50006
Cefn Goch (Merionethshire) 54005
Cefn Gwar y Felin (Breconshire) 47016
Cefn-llys (Radnorshire) 58006, 58007
Cefn Main (Denbighshire) 51018
Cefn ogo (Denbighshire) 51001
Cegidfa (Montgomeryshire) 56005, 56019
Cellan (Cardiganshire) 49003
Ceri (Montgomeryshire) 56001, 56017
Cerrigceinwen (Anglesey) 46006
Cerrigydrudion (Denbighshire) 51015, 51019
Ceulan-y-maes-mawr (Cardiganshire) 49008
Chirk (Denbighshire) 51016
Churchstoke (Montgomeryshire) 56001, 56003, 56004
Chwitffordd (Flint) 52022
Cilcain (Flint) 52002
Cilcennin (Cardiganshire) 49014
Cilrhedyn (Carmarthenshire) 50005
Cilwych (Breconshire) 47018
Clap Llanerch (Montgomeryshire) 56007
Clawdd-coch (Carmarthenshire) 50004
Cleirwy (Radnorshire) 58008
Cletterwood (Montgomeryshire) 56018
Cleviston Common (Glamorgan) 53009
Clocaenog (Denbighshire) 51005
Clogwyn (Caernarfonshire) 48011
Clyncothy (Carmarthenshire) 50018
Clynnog (Caernarfonshire) 48011
Clyro (Radnorshire) 58008
Cnwclas (Radnorshire) 58014
Cocks Furlong (Monmouthshire) 55008
Coed Marcham (Denbighshire) 51013
Coed-pen-maen (Glamorgan) 53005
Coedtalog (Montgomeryshire) 56008
Coed Ystumgwern (Merionethshire) 54004
Coety Higher (Glamorgan) 53003, 53013
Coffronydd (Montgomeryshire) 56018
Coity Wallia (Glamorgan) 53003, 53013
Coleshill Fawr (Flint) 52005
Colfa, or Colva (Radnorshire) 58012
Colwinston (Glamorgan) 53004
Common Coed y Pane (Monmouthshire) 55004
Common Sea (Monmouthshire) 55009
Common Wood (Denbighshire) 51008
Cors Ddyga (Anglesey) 46005

Cors Fochno (Cardiganshire) 49012
Coychurch Higher (Glamorgan) 53003
Crane (Montgomeryshire) 56008
Creig Byther (Radnorshire) 58001
Cuttir Bodwredd (Anglesey) 46002
Cuttir Ty Mawr (Anglesey) 46002
Cwm, (Y) (Flint) 52014, 52017
Cwmcarfan, or Cwmcarvan (Monmouthshire) 55012
Cwmcast (Denbighshire) 51018
Cwmgilla (Radnorshire) 58015
Cwmhiraeth (Carmarthenshire) 50005
Cwm-iou (Monmouthshire) 55002
Cwmllechach (Breconshire) 47016
Cwmmins Bach (Carmarthenshire) 50025
Cwmmins Penyllwyd-coed (Carmarthenshire) 50016
Cwm Wood (Monmouthshire) 55009
Cwmynace Hill (Radnorshire) 58029
Cwmyoy (Monmouthshire) 55002
Cwmysgyba (Merionethshire) 54004
Cwnsyllt (Flint) 52005
Cwym Bailey Glase (Radnorshire) 58029
Cydweli (Carmarthenshire) 50008
Cyffin (Montgomeryshire) 56008
Cyffylliog (Denbighshire) 51005
Dee Estuary (Flint) 52003
Denbigh Green (Denbighshire) 51007
Deneio (Caernarfonshire) 48002
Derwen (Denbighshire) 51005
Deuddwr (Montgomeryshire) 56005
Discoed Hill (Radnorshire) 58009
Diserth (Radnorshire) 58010
Diserth (Flint) 52017, 52019
Disgoed (Radnorshire) 58009
Dodleston (Cheshire) Included in 52009 (Flint)
Doethie Camddwr (Cardiganshire) 49009
Doethie Pysgotwr (Cardiganshire) 49009
Dolbenmaen (Caernarfonshire) 48012, 48013
Dolchenog (Cardiganshire) 49005
Doldremont (Cardiganshire) 49006
Dolgellau, or Dolgelley (Merionethshire) 54002
Drenewydd, Y (Montgomeryshire) 56001
Drenewydd Gelli-farch (Monmouthshire) 55009
Drenewydd yn Notais (Glamorgan) 53009
Dymeirchion (Flint) 52021
Dyserth (Flint) 52017, 52019
Earlswood (Monmouthshire) 55009
Ednol (Radnorshire) 58005
Efenechdyd (Denbighshire) 51005
Eglwys-bach (Denbighshire) 51006
Eglwysilan (Glamorgan) 53005
Eglwys Newydd, Yr (Glamorgan) 53002
Eglwys-rhos (Caernarfonshire) 48004
Eifl, Yr (Caernarfonshire) 48011
Ellesmere (Flint) 52004

Elvell, Upper (Radnorshire) 58010
Ely (Glamorgan) 53002
Evenjobb (Radnorshire) 58011
Faenol (Merionethshire) 54007
Farrington (Radnorshire) 58015
Fenechdid, Y (Denbighshire) 51005
Fens Heath (Flint) 52006
Foel Gasydd, or Gasyth (Denbighshire) 51018
Forden (Montgomeryshire) 56006
Forest (Carmarthenshire) 50018
Forest (Monmouthshire) 55004
Forest Fach (Radnorshire) 58003
Fron (Montgomeryshire) 56006
Fron Hill (Radnorshire) 58029
Ffordun (Montgomeryshire) 56006
Fflint, Y (Flint) 52005
Gaer Fach (Breconshire) 47016
Gallteg fa (Denbighshire) 51013
Galltwen (Denbighshire) 51001
Gallt y felin wynt (Denbighshire) 51001
Garneddwen (Caernarfonshire) 48010
Garth (Merionethshire) 54004
Garth and Ystrad (Cardiganshire) 49009
Garthbrengi, or Garthbrengy (Breconshire) 47006, 47020
Gartheryn (Denbighshire) 51021
Garthgell (Montgomeryshire) 56012
Gladestry (Radnorshire) 58012
Glascwm (Radnorshire) 58013, 58019
Glasgarmon (Radnorshire) 58033
Globwll (Montgomeryshire) 56010
Glynbrochan (Montgomeryshire) 56014
Glyndyfrdwy (Merionethshire) 54003
Glyngynwidd, or Glyngynwydd (Montgomeryshire) 56014
Gogoian, or Gogoyan (Cardiganshire) 49009
Golden Mile (Glamorgan) 53004
Gollen, or Golon (Radnorshire) 58016
Goodwick (Pembroke) no number
Gorwydd (Cardiganshire) 49009
Goss Llyferin, or Gors Lleferin (Caernarfonshire) 48002
Goston (Glamorgan) 53006
Gottell-y-Wern (Merionethshire) 54004
Grange (Carmarthenshire) 50008, 50019
Great Heath (Glamorgan) 53002
Green Moor (Monmouthshire) 55007
Gronant (Flint) 52010
Guilsfield (Montgomeryshire) 56005, 56019
Gungrog Fawr (Montgomeryshire) 56018
Gwedir (Caernarfonshire) 51020
Gwenfô (Glamorgan) 53012
Gwern y go (Montgomeryshire) 56019
Gwern-y-mynydd (Montgomeryshire) 56004
Gwespyr, or Gwesbyr (Flint) 52010
Gwndy (Monmouthshire) 55007, 55009, 55010, 55011
Gwnnws (Cardiganshire) 49004, 49005

Gwydyr (Caernarfonshire) 51020
Gwyddelfynydd (Merionethshire) 54008
Gwyddelwern (Merionethshire) 54003
Gwyddgrug (Carmarthenshire) 50007
Gwyllt Common (Merionethshire) 54004
Gyffylliog, Y (Denbighshire) 51005
Gyrncoch, or Y Gurn Goch (Caernarfonshire) 48011
Habbatch Hill (Radnorshire) 58029
Haminiog (Cardiganshire) 49014
Hanmer (Flint) 52006
Harpton (Radnorshire) 58031
Haverfordwest (Pembrokeshire) 57009
Hawarden (Flint) 52007, 52008
Henallt (Breconshire) 47007
Hendy Bank (Radnorshire) 58007
Henfache (Denbighshire) 51021
Hengoed (Denbighshire) 51013
Henllan (Denbighshire) 51007
Herbert (Glamorgan) 53009
Heyop (Radnorshire) 58014
Himble Hill (Radnorshire) 58029
Hiraethog (Denbighshire and Caernarfonshire) 51020
Hirwaun (Glamorgan) 53001
Hob, Yr (Flint) 52009
Holt (Denbighshire) 51008
Holyhead (Anglesey) 46002
Hope (Flint) 52009
Hopton (Montgomeryshire) 56001, 56004
Horse Moss Green (Flint) 52006
Huntington Hill (Radnorshire) 58012
Hurdley (Montgomeryshire) 56003
Hyssington (Montgomeryshire) 56007
Hwllffordd (Pembrokeshire) 57009
Ifton, or Ifftwn (Monmouthshire) 55003
Iscoed (Radnorshire) 58023, 58025
Kelston (Flint) 52010
Kerry (Montgomeryshire) 56001, 56017
Kidwelly St Mary (Carmarthenshire) 50008
Kilken (Flint) 52002
Kilkewydd (Montgomeryshire) 56006
Kinnerley (Shropshire, formerly partly in Montgomeryshire) no number
Kinnerton (Flint) 52009
Kinnerton (Radnorshire) 58005
Knighton (Radnorshire) 58015, 58017
Knolton Bryn (Flint) 52016
Knowle Hill (Radnorshire) 58029
Knucklas (Radnorshire) 58014
Lampeter (Cardiganshire) 49006
Latch Rhos (Radnorshire) 58018
Leckwith (Glamorgan) 53002
Letterston (Pembrokeshire) 57002
Lightwood Green (Flint) 52016
Little Green (Flint) 52006
Little Heath (Glamorgan) 53002

Long Mountain (Montgomeryshire) 56006
Loughor (Glamorgan) 53007
Lower Gro (Montgomeryshire) 56006
Lydham (Shropshire) 56004
Lyons (Denbighshire) 51008
Llanaber (Merionethshire) 54004
Llanaelhaearn (Carnarfonshire) 48011
Llanandras (Radnorshire) 58009
Llananno (Radnorshire) 58016
Llanarmon Dyffryn Ceiriog (Denbighshire) 51021
Llanarmon Mynydd Mawr (Denbighshire) 51021
Llanarmon-yn-Ial (Denbighshire) 51009
Llanarthne, or Llanarthney (Carmarthenshire) 50009
Llanasa (Flint) 52010, 52011
Llanbadarn Fawr (Radnorshire) 58020
Llanbadarn Fynydd (Radnorshire) 58016
Llanbadarn Odwyn (Cardiganshire) 49013
Llanbadarn Trefeglwys (Cardiganshire) 49001, 49014
Llanbeblig (Caernarfonshire) 48010
Llanbed'r (Anglesey) 46007
Llanbedr (Merionethshire) 54004
Llanbedr-goch (Anglesey) 46008
Llanbedr Newborough (Anglesey) 46007
Llanbedr Pont Steffan (Cardiganshire) 49006
Llanbedrog (Caernarfonshire) 48008
Llanbedrycennin (Caernarfonshire) 48006
Llanbister (Radnorshire) 58016
Llanblethian (Glamorgan) 53011
Llanboidy (Carmarthenshire) 50028
Llan-crwys (Carmarthenshire) 50024
Llancynfelin (Cardiganshire) 49008, 49012
Llandaff, or Llandaf (Glamorgan) 53002
Llandanwg (Merionethshire) 54005
Llandebïe, or Llandebye (Carmarthenshire) 50009
Llandefeilog, or Llandefaelog (Carmarthenshire) 50011
Llandefeisant (Carmarthenshire) 50013
Llandegla (Denbighshire) 51009
Llandeglau, or Llandegley (Radnorshire) 58019, 58020
Llandeilo (Pembrokeshire) 57003
Llandeilo-fawr (Carmarthenshire) 50012, 50013, 50022
Llandevenny (Monmouthshire) 55007
Llandilofawr (Carmarthenshire) 50012, 50013, 50022
Llandilo Patria (Carmarthenshire) 50013
Llandinam (Montgomeryshire) 56015
Llandrindod (Radnorshire) 58020
Llandrinio (Montgomeryshire) 56005
Llandinol (Cardiganshire) 49004
Llandogo (Monmouthshire) 55007
Llandrillo-yn-Rhos (Caernarfonshire and Denbighshire) 48004
Llandudno (Caernarfonshire) 48004
Llandwrog (Caernarfonshire) 48009
Llandybie (Carmarthenshire) 50009
Llandyfaelog (Carmarthenshire) 50011
Llandyfaelog Fach (Breconshire) 47019, 47010

Llandyrnog (Denbighshire) 51010
Llandysilio (Anglesey) 46003
Llandysilio (Montgomeryshire) 56005
Llandysul, or Llandyssul (Montgomeryshire) 56001
Llanddarog (Carmarthenshire) 50010
Llanddeiniol (Cardiganshire) 49004
Llanddeiniolen (Caernarfonshire) 48007
Llanddew (Breconshire) 47008, 47009
Llanddewibrefi (Cardiganshire) 49001, 49009, 49013
Llanddewi-yn-Heiob (Radnorshire) 58014
Llanddewi Ystradenni (Radnorshire) 58016, 58018, 58020
Llanddewi'r-cwm (Breconshire) 47007
Llanddunwyd (Glamorgan) 53011
Llanddwywe (Merionethshire) 54004
Llanddyfnan (Anglesey) 46006
Llanedi (Carmarthenshire) 50015
Llanegwad (Carmarthenshire) 50001, 50020
Llaneilian (Anglesey) 46003
Llaneilian-yn-Rhos (Denbighshire) 51006
Llanelidan (Denbighshire) 51011
Llanelli, or Llanelly (Carmarthenshire) 50014, 50015
Llanelltud, or Llanelltyd (Merionethshire) 54006
Llanelwedd, or Llanelweth (Radnorshire) 58010
Llanenddwyn (Merionethshire) 54004
Llanengan (Caernarfonshire) 48002
Llanerchidol (Montgomeryshire) 56019
Llanerfyl (Montgomeryshire) 56008
Llaneurgain (Flint) 52015
Llanfachreth (Merionethshire) 54006
Llanfaelrhys (Caernarfonshire) 48001, 48002
Llanfaglan, or Llanfaglen (Caernarfonshire) 48009
Llanfair (Merionethshire) 54004
Llanfair-ar-y-bryn (Carmarthenshire) 50006
Llanfair Caereinion (Montgomeryshire) 56011
Llanfair Clydogau (Cardiganshire) 49010
Llanfair Dyffryn Clwydd (Denbighshire) 51005
Llanfair Llythynwg (Radnorshire) 58012
Llanfair Mathafarn Eithaf (Anglesey) 46008
Llanfair Pwllgwyngyll (Anglesey) 46008
Llanfechain (Montgomeryshire) 56009
Llanfechell (Anglesey) 46004
Llanferres (Denbighshire) 52002
Llanfihangel Aberbythych (Carmarthenshire) 50009
Llanfihangel-ar-arth (Carmarthenshire) 50007, 50016, 50018
Llanfihangel Bachellaeth (Caernarfonshire) 48008
Llanfihangel Cilfargen (Carmarthenshire) 50020
Llanfihangel Cwm Du (Breconshire) 47018
Llanfihangel Esceifiog (Anglesey) 46005
Llanfihangel Fechan (Breconshire) 47010
Llanfihangel Genau'r-glyn (Cardiganshire) 49008, 49011, 49012
Llanfihangel Glyn Myfyr (Denbighshire) 51012
Llanfihangel Gwynllwg (Monmouthshire) 55005, 55009
Llanfihangel Helygen (Radnorshire) 58023, 58025
Llanfihangel Hills (Denbighshire and Merionethshire) 51012

Llanfihangel Nant Melan (Radnorshire) 58022
Llanfihangel Rhos-y-corn (Carmarthenshire) 50018
Llanfihangel Rhydieithon, or Rhidithon (Radnorshire) 58021
Llanfihangel Rogiet (Monmouthshire) 55005, 55009
Llanfihangel Tre'r-beirdd (Anglesey) 46001
Llanfihangel Troddi (Monmouthshire) 55012
Llanfihangel-y-Creuddyn (Cardiganshire) 49005
Llanfihangel-ye-roth (Carmarthenshire) 50007, 50016, 50018
Llanfihangel-yng-Ngwynfa (Montgomeryshire) 56009, 56012
Llanfihangel-y-Pennant (Caernarfonshire) 48013
Llanfihangel Ysgeifiog (Anglesey) 46005
Llanfihangel-y-traethau (Merionethshire) 48012, 54005
Llanfillo, or Llanfilo (Breconshire) 47012
Llanfleiddan (Glamorgan) 53011
Llanfrothen (Merionethshire) 48012
Llanfwrog (Denbighshire) 51013
Llanfyllin (Montgomeryshire) 56010, 56012
Llanfynydd (Carmarthenshire) 50013, 50020
Llanfyrnach (Pembrokeshire) 57004
Llangadfan (Montgomeryshire) 56008
Llangadog, or Llangadock (Carmarthenshire) 50013
Llangadwaladr (Denbighshire) 51021
Llangaffo (Anglesey) 46005
Llangan, or Llan-gan (Glamorgan) 53006
Llanganten (Breconshire) 47011
Llangathen (Carmarthenshire) 50020
Llangatwg (Carmarthenshire) 50013
Llangefni (Anglesey) 46006
Llangeinwen (Anglesey) 46007
Llangeitho (Cardiganshire) 49013
Llangeler (Carmarthenshire) 50005, 50017, 50019
Llangelynnin (Merionethshire) 54002
Llangennech (Carmarthenshire) 50015
Llangernyw (Denbighshire) 51014
Llangïan (Caernarfonshire) 48008
Llangioython (Cardiganshire) 49004
Llangollen (Denbighshire) 51016
Llangolman (Pembrokeshire) 57003
Llangrallo (Glamorgan) 53003
Llangristiolus (Anglesey) 46005
Llangunnog (Carmarthenshire) 50021
Llangunnor (Carmarthenshire) 50010
Llangurig (Montgomeryshire) 56013, 56014
Llangwm (Denbighshire) 51015, 51017, 51019
Llangwyfan (Denbighshire) 51010
Llangwynyw (Montgomeryshire) 56011
Llangwyryfon (Cardiganshire) 49004
Llangybi (Monmouthshire) 55004
Llangyfelach (Glamorgan) 53008
Llangynfelyn (Cardiganshire) 49008, 49012
Llangynllo (Radnorshire) 58003, 58014
Llangynnwr (Carmarthenshire) 50010
Llangynog (Carmarthenshire) 50021
Llangystennin, or Llangwstenin (Caernarfonshire) 48004

Llanhari, or Llanharry (Glamorgan) 53011
Llanhedr (Anglesey) 46007
Llanidan (Anglesey) 46005
Llanidloes (Montgomeryshire) 56015
Llaniestyn (Caernarfonshire) 48008
Llanilar (Cardiganshire) 49004, 49007
Llanishen, or Llanisien (Glamorgan) 53002
Llanishen, or Llanisien (Monmouthshire) 55012
Llanismel (Carmarthenshire) 50008
Llanllawddog (Carmarthenshire) 50001
Llanllugan (Montgomeryshire) 56016
Llanllwchaearn, or Llanllwchaiarn (Montgomeryshire) 56001
Llanllyfni (Caernarfonshire) 48011
Llanllŷr (Radnorshire) 58023
Llanmerewig (Montgomeryshire) 56001
Llanmyrewig (Montgomeryshire) 56001
Llannerch Banna (Flint) 52004
Llan-non (Carmarthenshire) 50009
Llanrhaeadr-ym-Mochnant (Denbighshire) 51021
Llanrhaeadr-yng-Nghinmeirch (Denbighshire) 51018
Llanrhystud (Cardiganshire) 49004, 49014
Llanrug (Caernarfonshire) 48010
Llanrwst (Denbighshire) 51020
Llanrysted (Cardiganshire) 49004
Llansadwrn (Carmarthenshire) 50022
Llansaintfraid, or Llansanffraid (Breconshire) 47012
Llansanffraid (Cardiganshire) 49014
Llansanffraid (Montgomeryshire) 56009
Llansanffraid-ar-Ogwr (Glamorgan) 53003
Llansanffraid Glan Conwy (Denbighshire) 51006
Llansanffraid Glynceiriog (Denbighshire) 51016
Llansannor, or Llansanwyr (Glamorgan) 53011
Llansteffan (Carmarthenshire) 50021
Llansteffan (Radnorshire) 58004
Llanteague, or Llan-teg (Pembrokeshire) 57005
Llan Trewyn (Denbighshire) 51011
Llanwenny (Radnorshire) 58022
Llanwimp (Radnorshire) 58004
Llanwnda (Caernarfonshire) 48009
Llanwnda (Pembroke) no number
Llanwnnog (Montgomeryshire) 56015
Llanwyddelan (Montgomeryshire) 56001
Llanybydder, or Llanybyther (Carmarthenshire) 50018, 50023
Llanychaearn, or Llanych'aiarn (Cardiganshire) 49004
Llan-y-crwys (Carmarthenshire) 50024
Llanymynech (Denbighshire) 51021
Llanynys (Denbighshire) 51023
Llanyre (Radnorshire) 58023
Llawrbante (Carmarthenshire) 50025
Llech Fared (Denbighshire) 51018
Lledrod (Cardiganshire) 49004
Llechryd (Radnorshire) 58010
Llwyneliddon (Glamorgan) 53012
Llysfaen (Caernarfonshire, later Denbighshire) 51022

Llys-wen (Breconshire) 47013, 47014
Llywel (Breconshire) 47005
Llysin (Montgomeryshire) 56015
Maesyfed (Radnorshire) 58002, 58029
Magor, or Magwyr (Monmouthshire) 55006, 55007
Mainstone (Shropshire) 56004
Malltraeth (Anglesey) 46005
Manafon (Montgomeryshire) 56001
Manordilo (Carmarthenshire) 50012
Manorowen (Pembrokeshire) 57006
Mara Mota (Breconshire) 47008
Marloes (Pembrokeshire) 57007
Maypole (Montgomeryshire) 56007
Mechain Iscoed (Montgomeryshire) 56009
Mechain Uwchcoed (Montgomeryshire) 56012
Meifod (Montgomeryshire) 56005, 56009, 56012
Melenydd (Radnorshire) 58018
Meliden (Flint) 52012, 52013
Mellington (Montgomeryshire) 56004
Merthyr Cynog (Breconshire) 47016
Minera (Denbighshire) 51004
Minutes Common (Monmouthshire) 55005
Mitchel Troy (Monmouthshire) 55012
Mochdre (Montgomeryshire) 56017
Mochras Sands (Merionethshire) 54005
Moel Famau (Denbighshire and Flint) 51009
Moel Feliarth (Montgomeryshire) 56008
Moelfre (Denbighshire) 51001
Moel Gasyth (Denbighshire) 51018
Mold (Flint) 52013
Molleston (Pembrokeshire) 57008
Monachlogddu (Pembroke) no number
Monyrythen (Radnorshire) 58029
Morfa Abererch (Caernarfonshire) 48002
Morfa Cwtta (Caernarfonshire) 48009
Morfa Dinas Dinlle (Caernarfonshire) 48009
Morfa Felin (Merionethshire) 54005
Morfa Harlech (Merionethshire) 54005
Morfa Mawr (Caernarfonshire) 48002
Morfa Mawr (Merionethshire) 54004
Morfa Neugwl (Caernarfonshire) 48002
Morfa Rhuddlan (Flint) 52017, 52019
Morfa Seiont (Caernarfonshire) 48005
Morfa Towyn (Merionethshire) 54007
Mucklewick (Montgomeryshire) 56007
Mwynydd Buchan (Glamorgan) 53002
Myarth (Breconshire) 47018
Mynydd Bach (Breconshire) 47016
Mynydd Bach (Cardiganshire) 49001, 49014
Mynydd Bach (Monmouthshire) 55009
Mynydd Bach Pen uwch (Cardiganshire) 49015
Mynydd Bach Twrgwyn (Cardiganshire) 49015
Mynyddcover (Carmarthenshire) 50010
Mynydd Eiddole (Carmarthenshire) 50011

Mynyddfirnach (Breconshire) 47015
Mynyddkerrig, or Mynydd Cerrig (Carmarthenshire) 50010
Mynydd Llanbedr (Merionethshire) 54004
Mynydd Llanddewi (Cardiganshire) 49001
Mynydd Llanddyfnan (Anglesey) 46006
Mynydd Llanfihangel (Carmarthenshire) 50016
Mynydd Llansadwrn (Carmarthenshire) 50022
Mynydd Llech (Denbighshire) 51018
Mynydd Llwydiart, or Llwydiarth (Anglesey) 46006
Mynydd Mynytho (Caernarfonshire) 48008
Mynydd Tegeingl (Flint) 52022
Mynydd y Glew (Glamorgan) 53011
Mynydd-y-Graig (Caernarfonshire) 48002
Mynydd y Gwair (Glamorgan) 53008
Mynydol Cilan (Caernarfonshire) 48002
Nancwnlle (Cardiganshire) 49015
Nannau-is (-yr)-afon (Merionethshire) 54006
Nannau-uwch- (yr)-afon (Merionethshire) 54006
Nannerch (Denbighshire) 52018
Nantci (Denbighshire) 51018
Nantglyn (Denbighshire) 51024
Nantmel (Radnorshire) 58023, 58024, 58025, 58032
Nant Rhys Dyliw (Cardiganshire) 49005
Nant-y-cae (Cardiganshire) 49005
Narberth (Pembrokeshire) 57008
Nefyn (Caernarfonshire) 48011
Netpool (Cardiganshire) 49002
Nevin (Caernarfonshire) 48011
Newborough (Anglesey) 46007
New Chapel (Montgomeryshire) 56005
Newmarket (Flint) 52014
Newport (Monmouthshire) no number
Newton Down (Glamorgan) 53009
Newton Nottage (Glamorgan) 53009
Newtown (Montgomeryshire) 56001
Niwbwrch (Anglesey) 46007
Northop (Flint) 52015
Norton (Radnorshire) 58027
Overgorther (Montgomeryshire) 56001
Overton, or Owrtyn (Flint) 52016
Pannell (Flint) 52008
Pemboyr (Carmarthenshire) 50005
Pembrey (Carmarthenshire) 50008
Pembroke (Glamorgan) 53009
Penallt, or Pen-allt (Monmouthshire) 55012
Penarlâg (Flint) 52007,52008
Pen-boyr (Carmarthenshire) 50005
Pen-bre (Carmarthenshire) 50008
Pencarreg (Carmarthenshire) 50026
Pencelli (Breconshire) 47012
Pen-coed (Glamorgan) 53003
Pencraig (Radnorshire) 58011,58031
Pendeulwyn (Glamorgan) 53011
Pendine (Carmarthenshire) 50027

Pendoylan (Glamorgan) 53011
Penkelly (Breconshire) 47012
Penley (Flint) 52004
Pen-llin, or Penlline (Glamorgan) 53006
Penmorfa (Caernarfonshire) 48013
Penrhos (Caernarfonshire) 48002
Penrhosllugwy (Anglesey) 46001
Pentrobin (Flint) 52008
Pentraeth (Anglesey) 46006
Pen-tywyn (Carmarthenshire) 50027
Pen-y-cil (Caernarfonshire) 48002
Pen-y-rhiw goch (Merionethshire) 54004
Penystrywaid (Montgomeryshire) 56015
Picton (Flint) 52010, 52011
Pilleth (Radnorshire) 58026
Pistyll (Caernarfonshire) 48011
Plas Dinas (Montgomeryshire) 56009
Pool (Montgomeryshire) 56005, 56018, 56019
Portfield (Pembrokeshire) 57009
Prestatyn (Flint) 52012
Presteigne (Radnorshire) 58009
Pyllalai (Radnorshire) 58026
Radnor Foreign (Radnorshire) 58022
Radnor Forest (Radnorshire) 58028
Radnor,New (Radnorshire) 58002, 58029
Radnor,Old (Radnorshire) 58011, 58031
Readymead (Monmouthshire) 55008
Redwick (Monmouthshire) 55007, 55008
Roath (Glamorgan) 53002
Robertstone Wathen (Pembrokeshire) 57008
Rogiet (Monmouthshire) 55005, 55009
Rug, Y (Merionethshire) 54003
Rurallt,South (Radnorshire) 58003, 58034
Ruthin (Denbighshire) 51005
Rhaeadr Gwy (Radnorshire) 58030
Rhandirisa (Carmarthenshire) 50006
Rhath, Y (Glamorgan) 53002
Rhayader (Radnorshire) 58030
Rhiew (Radnorshire) 58013
Rhiw, Y (Caernarfonshire) 48002
Rhiwlas (Denbighshire) 51021
Rhos Anhuniog (Cardiganshire) 49014
Rhos Cilcennin (Cardiganshire) 49014
Rhos Cilrhedin (Carmarthenshire) 50005
Rhos Commins (Caernarfonshire) 48011
Rhosddu (Caernarfonshire) 48008
Rhos-fawr (Caernarfonshire) 48002
Rhosgwfil (Caernarfonshire) 48002
Rhoshirwaun (Caernarfonshire) 48001
Rhosliswal (Radnorshire) 58018
Rhos Llangeler (Carmarthenshire) 50005
Rhospeiran (Cardiganshire) 49005
Rhos Penboyr (Carmarthenshire) 50005
Rhos Pengwern (Caernarfonshire) 48009

Rhos Poeth Green (Flint) 52006
Rhosrûg (Caernarfonshire) 48010
Rhos, The (Radnorshire) 58034
Rhostïe (Cardiganshire) 49004, 49007
Rhosybiswel (Cardiganshire) 49014
Rhos y caeran (Merionethshire) 54004
Rhosycorn (Carmarthenshire) 50018
Rhos-y-Gad (Anglesey) 46008
Rhos-y-garth (Cardiganshire) 49007
Rhos y meirch (Anglesey) 46006
Rhuddalt (Merionethshire) 54004
Rhuddlan (Flint) 52017, 52019
Rhuthun (Denbighshire) 51005
Rhydins (Breconshire) 47011
Rhysllyn (Radnorshire) 58023, 58032
St Asaph (Flint) 52017, 52019, 52020
St Bride's Minor (Glamorgan) 53003
St Clears (Carmarthenshire) 50028
St David's (Pembrokeshire) 57010
St Harmon (Radnorshire) 58016, 58023, 58024, 58033
St Ishmael (Carmarthenshire) 50008
St Lythan's (Glamorgan) 53012
St Michael Cwmdû (Breconshire) 47018
Saltney (Flint) 52007
Sanclêr (Carmarthenshire) 50028
Sarnau (Breconshire) 47019
Scyborycoed (Cardiganshire) 49011
Shelve (Shropshire) included in 56007
Shirenewton (Monmouthshire) 55009
Smatcher Hill (Radnorshire) 58029
Soughton (Flint) 52015
Starling Bank (Radnorshire) 58003
Stemmy Heath (Flint) 52006
Strata Marcellina, or Stret Marcel (Montgomeryshire) 56005, 56019
Swansea (Glamorgan) 53010
Swydd Dinieithon (Neithon) (Radnorshire) 58020
Talach-ddu (Breconshire) 47017
Talley (Carmarthenshire) 50012
Talwen (Breconshire) 47020
Talwrn Green (Flint) 52006, 52009
Talwrn mawr (Anglesey) 46006
Talyllychau (Carmarthenshire) 50012
Talyvan, or Tal-y-fan (Glamorgan) 53011
Teirtref (Montgomeryshire) 56004, 56006, 56018
Templeton (Pembrokeshire) 57008
Tempsîter (Montgomeryshire) 56006
Tintern (Monmouthshire) 55012
Tir Abbot Ucha (Denbighshire) 51019
Tirymynach, or Tir-y-mynech (Montgomeryshire) 56005
Town Hill (Glamorgan) 53010
Towyn (Merionethshire) 54007, 54008
Towyn Abergele (Denbighshire) 52019
Towyn Hill (Flint) 52012
Towyn Trewan (Anglesey) no number

```
Traean-Mawr (Breconshire) 47005
Traeth Mawr (Caernarfonshire and Merionethshire) 48012
Traian Manor (Breconshire) 47005
Trallwng, Y (Montgomeryshire) 56004, 56019
Trebrys (Denbighshire) 51021
Trefdraeth (Anglesey) 46005
Trefeglwys (Montgomeryshire) 56015
Trefesgob (Monmouthshire) 55007, 55011
Treflan (Caernarfonshire) 48010
Trefyclo (Radnorshire) 58015, 58017
Tregolwyn (Glamorgan) 53004
Tregrug (Monmouthshire) 55004
Trelawnyd (Flint) 52014
Treletert (Pembrokeshire) 57002
Tre-lech a'r Bettws (Carmarthenshire) 50025
Treleck (Monmouthshire) 55012
Trelogan (Flint) 52010
Trellan (Denbighshire) 51021
Tremeirchion (Flint) 52021
Tre-os (Glamorgan) 53006
Tretower (Breconshire) 47018
Tretwr (Breconshire) 47018
Tre-wern (Montgomeryshire) 56018
Tryleg (Monmouthshire) 55010
Tyddewi (Pembrokeshire) 57010
Ty-gwyn (Cardiganshire) 49005
Tyndyrn (Monmouthshire) 55012
Tywyn (Merionethshire) 54007, 54008
Ugre (Radnorshire) 58018
Ugre,South (Radnorshire) 58001, 58014
Undy (Monmouthshire) 55007, 55009, 55010, 55011
Upper Hamlet (Carmarthenshire) 50003
Waun-y-Gaer (Caernarfonshire) 48006
Wain Dyval (Glamorgan) 53002
Wain y Gyfir (Breconshire) 47008
Warren Mountain (Flint) 52008
Waun, Y (Denbighshire) 51016
Waunfawr (Caernarfonshire) 48010
Waun Gilwen (Carmarthenshire) 50005
Waungynnydd (Carmarthenshire) 50022
Waun Isaf (Pembroke) no number
Waunllefrith (Carmarthenshire) 50011
Waunmeiros (Carmarthenshire) 50017
Wayntrellwyd (Carmarthenshire) 50010
Welshpool (Montgomeryshire) 56004, 56019
Welsh St Donats (Glamorgan) 53011
Wentwood (Monmouthshire) 55012
Wenvoe (Glamorgan) 53012
Werndridd (Radnorshire) 58013
Whitchurch (Glamorgan) 53002
Whitford (Flint) 52022
Whitigader (Carmarthenshire) 50001
Whitson (Monmouthshire) 55013
Whitton (Radnorshire) 58034
```

```
Wilcrick (Monmouthshire) 55007
Wolfpitts (Radnorshire) 58031
Wrexham, or Wrecsam (Denbighshire) 51004
Wyddgrug, Yr (Flint) 52013
Ynyscynhaearn ( Caernarfonshire) 48012
Ynys wyllt (Caernarfonshire) 48011
Ysceibion (Denbighshire) 51023
Ysgeifiog (Flint) 52018
Ysgubor-y-coed (Cardiganshire) 49011
Ystog, Yr (Montgomeryshire) 56001, 56003
Ystradowen (Glamorgan) 53011
Ystrad Rhondda (Glamorgan) 53001
Ystradyfodwg (Glamorgan) 53001
Ystyllen (Merionethshire) 54004
Ywchcoed (Radnorshire) 58023, 58024
```